SHUJAA'AH

BOLD
LEADERSHIP FOR
WOMEN OF THE
MIDDLE EAST

ANNABEL HARPER

SHUJAA'AH

First published in 2020 by

Panoma Press Ltd
48 St Vincent Drive, St Albans, Herts, AL1 5SJ, UK
info@panomapress.com
www.panomapress.com

Book layout by Neil Coe.

978-1-784529-27-7

DEDICATION

This book is dedicated to all the women of the
Middle East and North Africa

PRAISE FOR THIS BOOK

"Deep understanding of the MENA region, global crisis and the time we live in. Thoughtful and bold leadership experiments to thrive and achieve life balance and gender equality."

Lina Farajallah

Consultant, People Development and Project Management

"Shujaa'ah clarifies the meaning of 'leadership' more generally and for the women in the Arab world more specifically. This book is a must-read for women in leadership. The personal anecdotes used in the book serve as good examples to model one's own behaviour."

Maha Bin Hendi

Founder and Managing Partner, Maha Bin Hendi Law Firm

"In this thoughtful book, Annabel helped me challenge my own long-held unconscious bias towards gender inequality in the Arab world. Enlightening read for men."

Ghaleb Darabya

Mason Fellow, Harvard Kennedy School

Managing Director, Cambridge Leadership Middle East Associates

"A thoughtful insight into how the region differs in leadership with useful research woven in."

Anne Archer

Executive Coach, Facilitator and Mental Health at Work Specialist

ACKNOWLEDGEMENTS

I have a very long list of people to thank and appreciate for getting me this far and rooting for me. There are many friends and colleagues who have supported the book and given me valuable feedback. In particular, I would like to thank Lina Farajallah and Ghaleb Darabya for their advice, wisdom, encouragement, good humour and friendship. Thank you also to Maha Albwardy for her inspiration, Maha Bin Hendi for her steady encouragement, Anne Archer for her thoughtful thinking, and John Moore for his warmth and honesty.

I would also like to thank the women who gave me their time and their voices for the book: Her Highness Basma Al Said; Hana Al-Syead; Shaikha Ahmad; Hamda Alshamali; Alia Al Nabooda; Linda Al Ali, and all the women who contributed anonymously. There are many other kind women and men in the Middle East who have taken time to talk to me, which I very much appreciate.

Closer to home, I would like to thank my dearest brother Simon Tuite for his sharp Editor's eye and generally keeping me going. The biggest thanks of all are due to my beloved family, my tribe: Jessica, Patrick and Amy for cheering me on with love throughout and of course, my husband Sam whom I can never thank enough.

CONTENTS

INTRODUCTION

In the Middle East, the role of women has particular complexities when it comes to examining the increasing leadership opportunities which are now emerging in the region. Global debates about gender parity and gender politics have kept the subject of women and leadership at the forefront of business conversations. It continues to be a hot topic everywhere, and there is now growing interest in the Middle East about how women can take more advantage of the new business opportunities that are opening up to them. The pace of change in the region has been fast, and as more women come into the workforce, they are beginning to find their collective voice and are demanding equal opportunities on a much larger platform than previously.

Having met and worked with many amazing women in the region, I have always been a champion and supporter of their cause. I hope my book contributes to this. It has been written for all the women I have met and have yet to meet. I hope that men will enjoy reading it too. The Middle East has become a very special place for me, and I hope my perspective on this unique culture reflects the warmth, humour and spirit of all the men and women who have welcomed me into their world. The vibrancy and energy of Arab life and the complexities of a long and traditional history have created a fascinating backdrop to how business is done. The meeting of traditionalism and modernism has meant that leaders are having to revise previous styles of leadership. It is a golden opportunity for women of the Middle East to step into the conversation.

As part of my MA in Middle Eastern Studies in 2017, my dissertation research explored the impact of the United Arab Emirates Government initiatives for women and leadership.[1] In 2020, I wanted to write a book about what, if anything, had changed, not just in the United Arab Emirates but also in the wider Middle East region. I have made references to this 2017 study where relevant.

Women's voices needed to be at the heart of the book. The response to my request for women to share their thoughts and experiences was uplifting. Some were happy to be identified, and others preferred to remain anonymous, in which case I have used a pseudonym. All gave their permission to use either direct quotes or synthesise their comments. They are all nationals from the Middle East and North Africa region. I have made a few small corrections in English syntax but only for clarity where needed.

The views expressed are mine, and any references to other authors have been attributed. Any errors or omissions are mine alone.

شُجَاعَة

CHAPTER 1

UNDERSTANDING THE CULTURAL CONTEXT FOR WOMEN AND MEN

"Would you like some dates, biscuits, chocolate, tea, coffee or water?" At the start of nearly every meeting I have attended with clients in the Middle East, the opening question from my client will be along these lines. For my part, I will offer a gift of sweets, dates, chocolate or something similar, often from the UK or wherever I have travelled prior to the meeting. This is likely to be followed by something like, "How are you, and how is your family?" When I ask the same question of my client, they will usually say the family are fine, followed by *"Hamdullah"* meaning "Praise God" or "Thank God" in Arabic. If a family member is unwell and I offer my wishes for a speedy recovery, the response is likely to be *"Inshallah"* which means "God Willing" or "It's in God's hands".

In spite of the differences from country to country and state to state, having spent 20 years travelling in the region and meeting and working with many nationals, three themes are consistently present in all my interactions. These core elements are all of equal importance, and I refer to them as the 3 Fs: Faith, Family and Food. With this foundation, the culture of the Middle East has evolved in a special and unique way. The link between these three components is the relationships. In my experience, the key to doing business and making friends is all about how you approach the relationship. Build the relationship, build the trust and people will go out of their way to help you, support you, and make introductions which becomes reciprocal. They have to like you and get to know you first.

Although this book has been written specifically for women of the Middle East, I truly hope that men will also find it of interest. As a backdrop to the following chapters, I will also be looking at some of the finer details for comparisons and differences between countries in the region. I do not think you can look at the position of women and leadership in the Middle East without keeping in mind the history, the geopolitical situation, and the culture. For many people reading this, much may be familiar, but I also hope that there will be some new elements of interest for you. This region cannot be assessed in isolation either and needs to be contextualised as part of the global picture. The history of all nations is relevant when understanding how societies have evolved, and their cultures have developed.

I have worked internationally in many different countries and regions, and there are different notes in the Middle East. It may be that the culture is still so strong, and its grip has not yet been loosened in the same way in all parts of the region by the advances of modernism, revolution, global economies, conflict and so on. Whatever it is that has created this extraordinary, dynamic and complex place, it has drawn me in with fascination, curiosity and continuous enjoyable learning.

The geography

The complexities manifest themselves across the region, by country and by demographic and not least by geography. To begin with, there are approximately 22 countries or states in the region. This figure is sometimes lower or higher depending on which countries are included. The majority of the population would identify Arabic as their first language. The region also has different names. It is known generically as the Middle East but if the North African countries of Morocco, Algeria, Libya and Tunisia are included, the region is referred to as Middle East and North Africa (MENA). Within the regions there are also different areas with separate identities. The North African countries mentioned are sometimes referred to as the Maghreb. There is also Egypt; the Levant, which comprises Lebanon, Syria, Palestine, Jordan and Israel; and the Arabian Gulf countries which are Bahrain, Iraq,

Oman, Qatar, Kuwait, Saudi Arabia and the United Arab Emirates (UAE). These Gulf countries, apart from Iraq, are part of the Gulf Co-operation Council, known as the GCC. This political and economic alliance was formed in 1981. For clarity, the term Middle East is used in general here unless referring to specific areas and countries.

Faith and culture

Islam is the predominant religion in the Middle East and runs through most people's way of living and indeed their DNA. In the Arab world, Muslim Family Law has also dictated the role of women through the centuries and still has a considerable influence on how women are viewed and what is acceptable for them to do outside the family environment. For centuries, rules and regulations for everyone were designed and decided by men and to suit men, creating patriarchal societies throughout the region. Women had their place, and although they could inherit and divorce, they were seen as delicate. They needed to be looked after and provided for. Men were dominant and had the last word.

Many aspects of these patriarchal systems remain, especially in more traditional countries and families. The tenets of respect for elders, family and others is one of the key principles as well as continued appreciation of what is provided through the belief that "It is all in the hands of God". This belief can sometimes make difficult challenges easier to bear. It is the foundation of social interaction and many local businesses. Observant Muslims take time for prayers every day, and holy days dictated by the cycles of the moon are part of the annual calendar. The month of Ramadan is an opportunity for reflection, fasting during daylight hours, and celebrating the *iftar* meal at sunset with family and friends. It is also a time for many to do voluntary and charitable work for the less fortunate or those who are living alone, including providing the *iftar* meal. However, this religious belief is only one half of the cultural picture in the Middle East. The other half is Arab culture itself, and these elements are tightly interwoven and bound together. It is the way of life.

There are also tribal roots which are especially important in the GCC countries. According to Dr Steffen Hertog, Associate Professor in Comparative Politics at the London School of Economics, these states comprised mainly social groups of tribes and merchants.[2] Once these countries became oil-rich, the power in these groups was overtaken by the power of the state and the development of infrastructures which allowed governments gradually to take more control. Over time, tribal groups lost much of their political and economic power and autonomy. Nevertheless, tribal heritage can still be a definition of social identity in the region.

Historically, family has been the centre of people's lives in the Middle East, as it is in most parts of the world. What makes this geographical area different is that many families are surrounded, either in the same house, or in neighbouring houses, by the wider family, including grandparents, uncles, aunts and cousins, and married and unmarried siblings. Most families have several children. The tradition is often that sons, upon marriage, bring their new wife to live in the family enclave. Daughters usually leave home when they marry and move into their new husband's home. Children are cared for and nurtured by everyone in the household, not just their own parents. Overall the patriarchal roots still dominate, though less in some countries than others. Women of the household are highly regarded and respected. Most women have a voice in family decisions, regardless of whether they work outside the home or not.

As a consequence of these large family units, mealtimes are an opportunity to celebrate coming together, traditionally over lunch. Meals are a time to talk, discuss issues and share news. Visitors bring additional food to add to the table. It is a place for robust, loud and happy conversations. This culture of sharing is replicated in business and social interactions.

Gender equality

The issue of gender equality in MENA and a woman's right to education and the right to work has been a growing subject of debate for many years. Outside the region, in England for example, women's rights to work came about through the mandatory introduction of education for all women towards the end of World War II. The 1944 Education Act was passed through parliament to enforce schools to open their doors and provide free education to young girls as well as young boys. Education smoothed the way for young women to move into the world of work, though actually securing jobs had many challenges as well as the quality of the jobs themselves.

The situation in the Middle East has varied on girls' education in spite of a UN Declaration that all women in the region are entitled to have access to education. Overall, the quality of education varies considerably from country to country, and several of the current local conflicts have either halted education altogether or reduced the content and availability. There are differences in government approaches. In the UAE for instance, since the establishment of the seven states comprising the UAE in 1971, the founding ruler Sheikh Zayed bin Sultan Al Nahyan clearly articulated that there should be equality for women and men and encouraged education for women. This has meant that by the time young women complete their education, more women than men have completed tertiary education according to the World Economic Forum (WEF) 2020 Global Gender Equality Report. Yet it seems that once women start working, the pace of their career progression slows down and that of men speeds up.

In the 2020 WEF report, Iceland topped the global list for gender parity for the 11th year running.[3] By region, MENA was the lowest globally at 61.1% for gender parity. Within these figures, Israel ranks highest in the region and stands at 64th globally. The UAE is 2nd highest but ranks 120th globally. There is a workplace gap across the Middle East. Only 14% of companies are female-owned, 18% of women are in senior manager roles, and 36% are in senior roles. According to the WEF 2020 data, it will take MENA 140 years to achieve gender parity. This figure is only beaten by North America where, perhaps surprisingly, WEF indicate that it will take 151 years to achieve parity. The figure for Europe, as a comparison, is 54 years.

It is not just a problem in the Middle East. The kinds of job roles that women have tend to fall into certain categories too. Globally, 65% of jobs in people and culture are held by women. There is a consistent lack of women in STEM industries (science, technology, engineering and mathematics). These include disruptive technology, new technology, AI, robotics and genetic engineering. These are known as 'frontier roles', the pioneers who will drive the increasing world of digitisation further into what the WEF in 2016 named the Fourth Industrial Revolution. Women should be at the forefront of this too. They certainly have the talent.

According to the WEF 2020 report, political empowerment is lower in the region than anywhere else globally, but the average has nearly trebled since 2006. Improved health services mean that life expectancy is better for women now, except for Bahrain and Kuwait. What is important to remember here is that many countries in their current state are still very young. The pace of change in some of these countries has been phenomenal in a very short time. They are adjusting and adapting, sometimes because there is unity on the vision, sometimes because they have had to. The voices of the young cannot be ignored either; they want a say in the shape of their country and their futures.

The nature of decision making

In the early development of Muslim traditions, tribal elders would come together at *majlis*, or council, to meet and pass judgment on misdemeanours and neighbourhood disputes, as well as discussing philosophical topics. Only males were allowed to attend *majlis*. The females of the house could only provide refreshments and then would have to withdraw.

Interpretations of religious rules and social laws and regulations were also discussed and decided at these meetings.

Called *majlis* in the Gulf region and *diwan* elsewhere, this tradition still exists and has evolved into networking as well, exploring business opportunities, making introductions to friends and relatives, and talks from a special invited guest. Any male can drop in, even if the attendees are unknown to him. It is also a place where potential job opportunities are discussed. These meetings are still only for men, and an alternative for women does not exist as such. For many women, this sense of exclusion is discouraging because they are not getting the chance to expand their networks in the same way or hear about new openings in the job market. In my 2017 research, one of the young women I interviewed was irritated by the fact that the only way she could get to hear about possible prospects was through her father or her brother.[4]

Women are not only missing opportunities for new jobs. In some organisations, issues that arise during meetings with both men and women in attendance often do not get resolved during the meeting but later, when the men meet over coffee. Women are finding that by the time of the next meeting at work, the issue has been decided without their input. It is encouraging that the Ruler of Dubai, His Excellency Sheikh Mohammed bin Rashid Al Maktoum has introduced mixed-gender majlis for VIP visits to the UAE and during Ramadan.

Hana Al-Syead, from Saudi Arabia, is a leading voice in the drive for global gender parity. Formerly the Head of Diversity at Olayan Financing Company, she is the founder of Wujud, a social enterprise which focuses on the integration of women into global economies. Her work is recognised by the World Economic Forum and Harvard Business School. When I raised the subject of *majlis* with Hana, she maintained that the *majlis* system existed all over the world. In her view, the difference between men's and women's networking was more to do with the approach. *"Men network to advance, women (in general) network to socialise,"* she said. Globally, women have adapted to using their networks in a more business-focused way. In the Middle East, the culture has made this harder for some women to do.

Business networking events which are mixed gender are scarce, and for those women working in organisations, this continues to be a challenge. Even though some parts of Middle East society consider it inappropriate for women to discuss business, many women are looking for these kinds of conversations, learning about their field, hearing thought-leaders and sharing knowledge from everyone, not just from other women. Business conferences do provide this opportunity, but mixed gender business networking meetings regularly provide a better resource to build knowledge, share ideas and make good business contacts.

The patriarchal nature of Arab society means that more often than not, fathers have been the decision makers about what their sons and daughters do. This has meant that once fathers started to accept the value of education for their daughters, they have been prime movers in encouraging their daughters into education. To some extent, rather than focusing on who their daughters marry, it has become 'education first' in many families. This has included travelling abroad for education, even if in the more traditional households women have had to be accompanied by their mothers or another female or male member of the family while they study.

Many women who seek further education overseas have a sense of getting experience and then 'giving back' to their nation. This also applies to the kind of organisations they are working in. Some seek out jobs in multi-national corporations (MNCs) in the region to get exposure to global business and bring that experience back into local organisations or set up their own businesses. Rather than fathers, it is sometimes mothers and brothers who have had to adjust to this. They worry about the risk to 'making a good marriage' if young women are better educated than their husbands.

As in many countries globally, when Middle East women went into the workplace, it was into the 'caring' professions: teaching, nursing or general medical practice. For a long time, these were often the only option. Law and accountancy became more acceptable, and now women are training in a broad range of disciplines including financial services, engineering, pilots, leading innovation and smart technology projects, and specialist sciences. Many women are aspiring to become the first female

Emirati astronaut, now that the UAE has developed its own space programme.

The position of men

The growing call for women's equality in the Middle East poses potential challenges for men, and it has not been an easy adjustment for individuals and for society as a whole. As more women seek progression in their careers, they can be perceived as a threat to their male colleagues. If they are more successful as well, it makes matters worse because of the perceived impact on their status at work. Status is an important attribute in Arab culture, and to lose it can engender a great sense of shame. Shame has a huge impact, particularly with men. Public shame and the engulfing sense of humiliation can be difficult to combat, and in Arab culture it will be seen as failure.

Arab men are hard-wired to be strong and capable. It is a reflection of their upbringing. Sons are often treated as the special ones or the favourites, that they will be the providers for their own families. In addition, they are brought up with expectations that women will obey them and do as they are told. Mistakes are brushed aside, and as a consequence, they do not learn to fail. Failure means letting their families down, and I have worked with clients who have had a failure or a problem which they have not shared with their families. One of my male coaching clients from the Middle East had not told his wife or family that he had not achieved the promotion he was seeking. Another client worked for his family's professional services business which had been founded by his grandfather. He felt trapped by the responsibility to uphold the family name but hated his job and had absolutely no interest in finance. He loved to cook and what he really wanted to do was to open a restaurant. When I asked him why he had not told his family, he said it would be devastating for his mother and would bring shame on her and the family.

A sense of shame may also be felt when people are moved out of one job into another, or from one department to another. Government entities, particularly in the GCC, are notorious for moving those who are perceived to be poor performers from one ministry to another. They are not given any feedback; they are just moved. They are often given a different title as a way of saving face or describe their new role in a way that helps them to save face. It may also be that a male manager feels shame when a female in a lower ranking role is promoted over him.

This goes back to the expectations for that man growing up and his family environment, which encouraged him to feel that he would be entitled to promotions, success at work and superiority. Even younger men are not always comfortable with a female manager, and whilst they are fine with their wife-to-be working before marriage, they find it difficult to tolerate after they are married.

One Middle Eastern coaching client of mine had a sophisticated background and had been well educated abroad. He had witnessed many situations internationally, where both husbands and wives worked. Nevertheless, he was adamant that his wife would not work as it would be a reflection on him. He would be seen as not earning enough to support her, and this would be shaming for him.

Organisational demographics

The organisations I refer to in this book are of all and any kind across any industry and line of business. They might be large corporates, small independent companies, boutique firms, family-owned businesses, public sector, educational institutions and so on. I am using the term as a catch-all for any entity, even if it is solo-owned, so long as there is a leadership role within it. Leadership and personal development programmes exist, but there is not a consistent pattern. MNCs often provide better training and development opportunities which women can take advantage of. My sense is that this is because they are happening in other parts of the business outside the region, so there is an existing culture which supports personal development.

Statistically, the numbers of expatriate and national population in the GCC is roughly balanced. However, in certain countries, the expatriate community far outweighs the local population. For example, in the UAE, nearly 90% of the population is expatriate.[5] In spite of the overall number of expatriates, the vast majority of public sector jobs are held by nationals. They are considered safe, supported by government and tend to have better hours. They have also guaranteed a 'job for life' which means that many posts are held by older people who have been in their organisations for a long time and are causing a bottleneck in terms of career progression for those who joined later. For women, public sector jobs are seen to be particularly attractive as they are more 'family-friendly' and have shorter hours.

Public sectors in MENA are key employers for nationals, especially women, and this region has some of the largest public sectors globally. However, the employment figures vary in one significant aspect. Across the GCC countries, approximately 75% of the national workforce are employed in this sector. Outside the GCC, the figure reduces by nearly half.[6] This presents a challenge in the current job market because recruitment in the public sector has slowed and some existing roles are held by people who have been in the sector for many years which has not created much room for upward career progression.

The increased pressure on oil-producing countries to find other ways to sustain their economies, plus the drop in recruitment in the public sector, has put the spotlight firmly on the private sector to create more opportunities for nationals. Several Gulf countries have introduced a policy to push for more national employees to be represented across all sectors, and in some cases, new jobs can only be offered to nationals. They have priority. Examples of this are 'Saudization' in the Kingdom of Saudi Arabia, 'Emiratisation' in the UAE and 'Omanisation' in Oman. This is enabling young women who are nationals to apply for jobs they may not have considered previously, in spite of their high standard of education and qualifications.

This applies equally to local companies which currently employ expatriates. Financial packages for foreigners usually come with premium rates and benefits and are tax-free. Across the region, the advent of the Fourth Industrial Revolution will mean a drive to reduce costs and increase efficiency. More women need to be brought into leadership roles at this critical time, to increase diversity and inclusion. Organisations need to capture this resource and use the strengths of both women and men to make their companies fit for the future.

The career path for women

For women in MENA, first and second jobs once they begin working can progress well. However, once they reach mid-level, the statistics look very different according to the WEF 2020 Global Gender Equality report. The divergence between their education and their seniority is significant. By the time women reach junior manager roles, progression often slows down, and they can become the 'squeezed middle'. This is particularly relevant in the public and government entities. It might be the so-called glass ceiling – some may even call it a concrete ceiling – but with added complexity for three main reasons.

Firstly, male colleagues have been working for longer and have moved into senior roles. They tend to stay there. This particularly applies to locally owned and based organisations. As already mentioned, development programmes are thin on the ground, so acquiring skills like influencing and negotiation, managing difficult conversations, and leadership courses are not available to many women or men. The purse-holders tend to be at CEO level. They are often men and some, though by no means all, have traditional views on a woman's role and are not willing to change that view. Women may marry and start families during this stage of their lives as well. They want to tend to their children as well as work, and in traditional families, this is expected. In some organisations, the culture is not conducive to part-time working, job share or shorter hours. Women often gravitate to jobs in the public sector, especially if they have young families. The hours are shorter, so they finish work earlier. Women may take a break to spend time at home. They are often not taken seriously when they return to work by some of their male colleagues, who think they should be at home anyway and not working at all.

Secondly, it is important to remember that in Arab culture, everything to do with business begins with relationships. If someone likes and trusts you, they will do business with you and go out of their way to make introductions to help you. Business relationships across the world are formed by and large through networks, connections and introductions. New hires are often people who have been approached or 'tapped on the shoulder'. In the Middle East, the bond of family and kinship means these connections often run much deeper. In the past, new hirings were often based on family and tribal connections, known as *wasta* in Arabic. This system still prevails. Not only does it put potential candidates higher up the list, but it also means they can be exposed if they fall short.

Finally, one of the known routes to making connections, building skills and business knowledge is through mentoring schemes. Opportunities for mentoring are not consistent across many male-dominated organisations. Mentoring is usually carried out by someone more senior than the mentee, and available mentors are likely to be male. There are cultural aspects to manage: by their nature, mentoring conversations are held in a private space and for some, a male colleague meeting with a female colleague alone, even at work, is unacceptable.

Even if there is a mentoring scheme available, some people are set in their view that women should not be focusing on their careers first, but their families first, and it is often difficult to find mentors in some local organisations. By the same token, some women are put off the idea of mentoring because they feel they will be judged and cannot be open in the conversation. MNCs tend to facilitate mentoring more, and this is especially likely in those companies that already run mentor schemes in their other businesses outside the region. If there is no official mentoring scheme, some women seek out a mentor on an informal basis to support them in their careers.

In some organisations, there has been a slight increase in senior women mentoring juniors. Women are slowly being recruited to join boards of large and complex organisations. Others have become CEOs. They are role models for young women, as are some of the leading women who are now getting involved in politics.

As more young people start their careers, this will change many of the dynamics in organisations in the Middle East. The mistake that many leaders are making right now is trying to fit these young people into their own current reality, instead of trying to forge a new way of going which both the young and the existing leadership need to adjust and adapt to. One opportunity to help grow a better understanding of the generations is what is known as 'reverse' mentoring. Rather than an experienced, usually older and certainly more senior, member of the firm mentoring a younger, less experienced employee, it can work both ways. The digital literacy and understanding of their world mean that this younger demographic has a lot of existing knowledge which can be tapped into. Senior people can benefit from this knowledge. It keeps their fingers on the pulse of business, not just their own but also that of their competitors. They can feed this learning back into the organisation at the most senior levels.

Several countries have women at senior levels of government including Lebanon, Morocco, Tunisia, Algeria, Oman, Bahrain, Saudi Arabia and the UAE. But there is still opposition to women holding senior roles. The appointment in 2020 of eight senior women prosecutors to the role of judges in Kuwait, the first time women have been appointed to this role, was heavily criticised by some of the more traditionalists in the country who felt that only men have the mandate to be judges. Nevertheless, these role models and the equality of education means that younger women are beginning to realise that they can also achieve more senior roles. They see what is possible and see no reason why it should not be available to them too.

Women entrepreneurs

One area of business which has seen tremendous growth is amongst women entrepreneurs in the Middle East. It may well be that the root of this lies in the fact that women have been able to develop small businesses of their own based at home. They have been able to secure a family loan to help set themselves up, and whilst working, they are still under the eye of male members of the family. Early entrepreneurial businesses tended towards home products or fashionwear and were aimed at women. Customers visit during the day in an area of the house that is exclusively female. These kinds of businesses are still flourishing, but alongside these there has been a massive growth in other types of businesses, including all-women law firms, architectural design, financial services for women, events organisers and large fashion houses. Many female entrepreneurs have had financial support from their families, which means that male members of the household still hold the purse-strings and have ultimate financial control. However, this does not apply to everyone. Some women have had to fight hard to make their own way and build not just their own financial independence, but also generate enough income to support their families.

I came across the story of a married Jordanian woman who lived in a conservative area in Amman, where few women go out to work. They also cannot receive male guests in the home without their husbands being present. The issue for Maryam Mutlaq involved getting repairs arranged, including plumbing. Sometimes weeks might go by until problems like leaking pipes could be fixed because she was dependent on her husband being able to get a day off work to be at home when the plumber called. In 2014, through a US government aid initiative and encouraged by her husband, Ms Mutlaq enrolled in a training course for plumbers. Eventually, she set up a training project to train other women and opened a plumbing shop. Ms Mutlaq is a fine example of reaching for innovative solutions, sticking to her goal and being single-minded. It is an important mindset to develop if you want to reach your goal of being a leader.

These women business owners are mentoring others who are developing their own businesses. They have also created networks for entrepreneurial women, often with speakers to give advice on running a small business and to make introductions. Nevertheless, in Jordan and Iraq, fewer than 15% of women are working and only 26% in Lebanon. Current economic challenges in those three countries could be having an impact. However, there are barriers to women entering the labour market, including being married and having a family. The opposite is true for men.

There is one sobering thought to keep in mind in spite of some of these initiatives towards gender equality. Violence against women is a global problem. In 2020, 45% of women in the Middle East experienced some kind of violence against them – the highest regional figure globally.[7] As a comparison, the figures for the US were 32%, and 22% in Western Europe. The overall global figure was 31%. In July 2020, thousands of women held a protest in Amman, Jordan following a series of so-called honour killings. They were demanding a change in the law which protected perpetrators and appealed to the government to abolish the statute. Global organisations such as the World Health Organisation, the World Bank and the United Nations also expressed concerns about the rising numbers globally of domestic violence during the 2020 pandemic caused in part by lockdown. The pandemic also stalled or put back many advances in gender equality, some of which were very hard won.

شُجَاعَة

CHAPTER 2

THE WORLD IS CHANGING

The Coronavirus pandemic of 2020 catapulted an already changing world into a whole new environment. Short-term impacts quickly became measurable in terms of loss of life, global economies shrinking, lost businesses and disruption to everyone's familiar way of living and working. The predictable nature of life prior to the pandemic changed. The truth is that the 21st century, even before the end of its first decade, had ushered in increased terror attacks on a global scale causing a large number of fatalities in different parts of the world, and a global recession which lasted nearly two years and caused the loss of many businesses and a dramatic rise in global unemployment.

Post 2010, technology began to develop beyond imagination, and this development has been one of the great disruptors of how business is done in many parts of the world. It continues to evolve at great speed. Many traditional businesses, for instance in banking, have become successful and agile fintech organisations. Business has changed already and will continue to do so as digital advances grow. Automated factories are using the latest AI technology; doctors can treat patients thousands of miles away using virtual communication, and family and friends can keep in regular contact virtually regardless of their location. Digital technology is changing the face of leadership as well as how organisations work. Unless organisational leaders take this on board and develop an entrepreneurial mindset throughout their organisations, some businesses will not survive, and those businesses which do not already have at least one Chief Technical Officer are unlikely to succeed.[8] This, coupled with the after-effects of the pandemic, means that we need good leadership in organisations more than ever before.

Definitions of leadership

What does leadership mean to you? If you type 'definitions of leadership' into Google, on any given day, you are likely to get more than a billion hits! How do you want to show up as a leader? Certainly it means being able to adjust quickly to fast-changing environments in an uncertain world. The acronym VUCA, meaning volatility, uncertainty, complexity and ambiguity was first coined by Bennis and Nanus in 1987.[9] It is particularly relevant now in the 21st century even though we are only a fifth of the way through it.

Status and titles in the Middle East carry a lot of weight. Consider this when you think about leadership. Is it about the role or title? Is it about what you will do in that role? Can you be a junior leader, with a team of two direct reports? Or does being a leader mean making it to the senior management team or CEO? The terms leadership and management are often interchangeable. Definitions of what being a leader means and what a manager means also depend on title styles in different organisations. A manager in one company might be at a relatively junior level with maybe one or two direct reports or even none. In others, a manager will have a wide range of responsibilities and several direct reports.

In the US and Europe, you will often hear discussions from leadership specialists about leadership traits, behaviours, styles, and how leadership is about building the organisation, creating a culture which enables trusting relationships, accountability and responsibility. Academics have conducted endless research on what it means to be a good manager and what it takes to be a good leader. Leaders must take responsibility and be accountable.

Having the title of leader may add some authority to the individual, but it is no guarantee that the individual is or will be a great leader of others. In the theory of Adaptive Leadership, there is a difference in leaders who rely on the authority of their title to lead and those who use their role to lead well, especially through change.[10] This is the moment not only to address the technical challenges of a problem – the 'task'; it is also the time to look at the adaptive challenge involved. What needs to be done to find a new way of going, which means bringing the best of what has been done previously, stop doing what is no longer fit for purpose, and create a new way of operating? This requires engaging people in the organisation to embrace the changes with head and heart, co-creating new meaning and purpose at work. Without this approach, implementing change that is sustainable will not happen.

Leadership can also be defined by impact, not just on the bottom line, but also on the values and ethics of the company. This will feed directly, in a positive or a negative way, into how much each employee feels their work has meaning and purpose. Some of these definitions could be considered to be fairly generic and fixed in the traditional Western approaches to leadership. They have a value, but in the Middle East there are additional nuances which should be considered when looking at leadership and what it means. Islamic faith is the central pillar of the Arab belief system. Consequently, many principles defining how people live their lives also apply to the way people do business and how local companies in different countries are organised.

Virtual working

One of the many reflections organisations need to make now is how to engage a workforce that is working virtually. A manager may be located in one country, with direct reports spread globally. Virtual working is not just confined to global organisations either. A central skill of leadership is forging and maintaining connected relationships in the organisation. Microsoft founder Bill Gates revealed in an end-of-year blog in 2018 that one of the questions he asked himself to check on his quality of life was, "Did I develop new relationships and deepen old ones?"[11] As an older man, he acknowledged that he would never have asked himself that question in his 20s. Even the driving force behind Apple, the late Steve Jobs, who was passionate about the digital world, insisted that meetings were face to face. According to his biographer, Jobs felt that creativity grew out of the contact with others in arranged conversations and also happened in informal ways just by chance meetings. One of his leadership rules was ensuring that everyone had face to face meetings rather than virtual.[12]

It can be isolating, and difficult to feel engaged and motivated if you are based in a location thousands of miles away from head office with no regular face to face contact with your boss or even other work colleagues. This was already one of my biggest concerns about virtual working. There are business benefits for those companies who spend big budgets on air travel. It is the amount of virtual working that is worrying. Evidence is building about how the effect of constantly working in a virtual world with little human contact is affecting mental health and wellbeing through the experience of the Covid-19 pandemic.

When the pandemic began to take hold in 2020, this was especially evident in the coaching engagements I had with clients across the MENA region. As already stated, Arab culture is very sociable. The pleasure of these social interactions was cut short. The sense of loss of such a fundamental aspect of day to day life was particularly acute. One client had been trapped by a ban on flights from the country where he was working. During that time, he became depressed and felt increasingly isolated. His family lived in another part of the Middle East, and it took several weeks before he was able to travel home.

New opportunities for women

The advent of rapidly evolving technology has created opportunities for women in the Middle East, not just in their work. It has also given them the chance to speak out and claim more independence as a result of the explosion in social media and their access to it. It has provided a window to what is possible. There is a greater awareness in the Middle East than ever before about what is happening in other countries. Young women and men from the region expect to have the same opportunities as their global contemporaries. Many of these women want to have successful careers and are highly educated.

In some countries where daughters have traditionally stayed at home until marriage, some of these daughters are beginning to move out and set up home alone. It may take a while to persuade the family. One young woman I met in a GCC country had a job in one city and lived in another one, which meant her drive to and from work took up a long part of her day. She managed to persuade her family that moving to the city where her job was would help her to manage her energy better. Eventually, her parents agreed, with the proviso that she would always return home at the weekend. She was confident that in time, she would be able to negotiate agreement that she could stay in her apartment during some weekends. Her parents' reluctance was not about being deliberately obstructive. They were concerned about her safety, what other people might say about her and how it might reflect on them because it was so unusual.

More women are also finding the confidence to leave an unhappy marriage and set up home with their children. In traditional Middle East societies where men see their role as nurturers and carers of the female members of the family, it can be a hard transition for women to make and takes a lot of courage. It would have been unheard of until relatively recently and would have brought shame on the family. Divorce figures, particularly in the GCC, are steadily rising year on year as more women are finding their own voices.[13]

Population changes in the Middle East

There has been an enormous rise in the population of under 35s all over the region. According to a World Bank report in 2020, 60% of the population was under 30. Many younger women are demanding to be treated as equal to their male peers.

This generation has a well-developed sense of what their expectations are in life. They see the impact the 2008 recession has had on their lives and do not want to repeat the same patterns. They embrace the advances in technology and are at ease working digitally. I find their energy and enthusiasm extremely uplifting and encouraging. Aspirations to follow the traditional career paths in many organisations – the career and job for life approach – is no longer relevant or even applicable. There can be no such certainty.

Globally people are living longer. Rather than a job for life, the standard is more likely to be a portfolio career with experience of a wide variety of roles and businesses. Many of these young people have witnessed the fall-out in family relationships from job obsession. Their choice is to have a balance: spend time at work and also time out, socially and in their own special relationships. They do not want to compromise. Their world view will often encompass the importance of personal health and wellbeing, eating the right food and keeping fit. Corporate social responsibility and sustainability is a frequent topic in my coaching conversations. These are the leaders of tomorrow, and they want to shape their own destinies. They have the capacity to be mobile, adventurous, experimental and significantly, feel a great sense of responsibility to give back to their individual countries.

The rising number of young people in the population presents a considerable challenge for organisations. Some firms would like to hire young people and then put them on a career track, with the high potentials being offered a variety of training courses along the way. This used to be considered as a good investment for the future of the company over the following years. Now that globally people are living longer, there is the potential if desired or financially required to have a longer working life. Consequently, portfolio careers are becoming more popular. These are careers where someone might spend a few years in one kind of business and then move on to several different types of enterprise during their working life. Companies have started to question the investment in these training courses when people may move on to a role in another company in three to five years. There is capacity for women to seize the initiative here and go back into work if they have taken time out to raise their families.

Company culture

Companies change and evolve over time. It has always been the case that company culture draws most people into work. Inevitably, that company culture can change significantly even in a short period of years. What once seemed attractive and created aspirational ambitions to work in one particular organisation may change. The cultural environment may become uncomfortable. Given all the considerations that younger people are giving to their lives both at work and outside, this cultural fit and meaning and purpose of working in one job or another has become even more central to their choices. If the culture and values of the organisation do not appeal, it will not be a good fit, and the same applies if those values change or are no longer congruent with personal values. Purpose is personal, but if employees can feel attached to the values of the organisation and its purpose, then they will find meaning and purpose *for themselves* and will feel more committed to working there. This applies as much to working in the Middle East as it does anywhere else.

Meaning and engagement can be harnessed by permission to experiment, make mistakes, try different things, feel challenged, and learn. In 2012, Google began a long-term study to discover the ingredients of a successful team. Named 'Project Aristotle' they found that the most important aspect was creating psychological safety. This means that team members feel comfortable about taking risks, coming up with ideas and making mistakes which will not be held against them. They are not worried about showing their vulnerability.[14] Humans are social creatures. A sense of belonging is just as important at work as it is at home – honest, open and trusting lines of communication oil the wheels.

That sense of belonging was one of the toughest social challenges of the 2020 pandemic. Social isolation during this time proved to be a serious problem for many people who may already have been vulnerable. There is growing concern in the Middle East about mental health. It has a stigma, and many people feel ashamed to talk about it. Mental health services vary widely in the region. The younger generation is of particular concern, according to a psychologist based at the German Neuroscience Centre in Dubai. They are more aware of what is going on in the outside world and consequently have higher expectations which may not be met. They also have less resilience to deal with it.[15]

Open communication about personal problems is not always apparent in organisations that I have worked with, particularly with regard to making mistakes and the sense of shame if things go wrong. The culture makes it difficult to ask for help, and showing your weaknesses can feel risky.

As I have found in many coaching sessions, it is not because clients do not want to discuss sensitive issues, it is more about feeling that they cannot ask for help according to custom. Coaching is an opportunity to talk openly in a safe and confidential space. I am not part of Arab culture, but I do understand it. I have been privileged to witness some significant positive changes in clients in these situations.

Progress on equal rights

Some of the countries in the region already have equal rights to jobs with no distinctions between male and female applicants. However, in those countries where opportunities for more freedom and equal rights have slowly developed for women or have very recently begun to emerge, there has been an exponential growth in women in the job market. Saudi Arabia is one notable example. Recent developments in the Kingdom have included allowing women to drive, and they can now leave the country without a male guardian or male relative's permission. The Saudi government has recently appointed 13 women to the Human Rights Council, which now has a 50/50 gender split.

Some Middle East observers may be surprised by this. The opening up of the country needs to be seen in the light of its history. It is still a conservative country, but there is now a recognition that changes need to come. Women have longed for these opportunities, and these numbers will grow. Now that they have this empowerment, it will only expand, not shrink.

It could be argued that those governments who have been slower to bring equal employment rights to women may have had changes forced on them by the increased awareness of inequalities and the growing global conversation about gender equality. Governments have had to take a stand and be seen to do so. They have been quick to raise awareness about what they are implementing. This has created a situation in which women could take more advantage. They now have visible, publicly articulated government backing.

شُجَاعَة

CHAPTER 3

EQUAL PAY, BOARDS AND GOVERNMENT INITIATIVES

The United Nations Charter was adopted by all its members in 1945. Included in the Charter was agreement that there should be equal rights for men and women and that the responsibility to ensure that women had those rights lay with each member country and state. More than 70 years after that declaration, this mission statement has still not been met in every part of the world.

Although data may indicate that things have improved, there is plenty of evidence anecdotally and through academic research that this is not necessarily the case at ground level in many women's experiences. This includes not being taken seriously at job interviews, unconscious bias when recruiting women into organisations, professions not being flexible with childcare where a woman might be the only caregiver, and limiting choices of jobs to the caring professions, such as health workers at junior levels, and teaching. As has already been mentioned, most notably the pay gap between women and men globally is still too wide.

The trouble with equal pay

Equal pay for equal work has been a contentious issue in many countries. Even where equal pay legislation has been introduced, there are still considerable gaps. For example, in the UK, the Equal Pay Act was passed into British law in 1970. It stipulated that there should be no distinction between men and women regarding pay and conditions. 2019 figures showed that women's pay lagged behind that of their male counterparts by 17.3%.[16] Although women in the UK account for half the population, at best they represented roughly 25% of jobs in law, just under 30% of jobs in business, and around 25% of the political establishment.

Women are good at negotiating on behalf of their teams and are more successful than men in achieving better salaries, conditions and organisational commitment to improvements. However, when they enter into negotiations for themselves regarding pay, bonuses, equal recognition and so on, they tend not to be so successful. In 2018 in the European Union, women's hourly rate of pay was on average 14.8% lower than their male colleagues.[17] Research carried out in 2003 by Professor Linda Babcock and her colleague Sara Laschever showed that women tended not to ask for pay rises because they were being 'good' girls and expected to be rewarded for working hard.[18] On the other hand, men were prepared to initiate salary discussions and frequently received an increase in pay as a result. Babcock and Laschever also observed that in some organisations, women were not being offered higher wages because of the stereotypical view that women are more accommodating and therefore would not challenge their level of pay.

Some of the resistance against women negotiating for a higher salary is connected to societal views that women are the carers and should not strive to seek individual gain. Researchers found that in the Middle East this perception is heightened because Arab women are expected to be modest and not interested in material gains.[19]

In 2017, a case of organisational bias surrounding women's pay negotiations came to light very publicly at the BBC at its London headquarters. The BBC had been forced to publish the salaries of their highest earners in their Annual Report. The figures showed that the highest earning journalists were all men. Women journalists formed a coalition to fight this imbalance and one of them, Carrie Gracie, resigned from her post as China Editor having learned that two male colleagues in equivalent roles were earning 50% more than she was in spite of the parity of job description and responsibilities. The BBC eventually acknowledged that there had been an unfair gap in her pay and awarded her more than £300,000 sterling in back pay. She donated the payout to a charity which campaigns for women's rights and gender equality. Another female presenter discovered she was also earning a lot less than her male colleagues, although she was performing the same role with the same responsibilities. The BBC later apologised and awarded her a substantial six-figure sum. Some of her male colleagues took a pay cut so that their salaries equated to hers. But that was not really the point. The BBC had managed, either by intention or through unconscious bias towards female journalists, to negotiate lower fees with their female presenters.

Although the public airing of these problems at the BBC was hard for the women involved and caused them considerable stress, by not raising the issue it would have given a different message to the people they were working with, both men and women. This is why this story matters. Acquiescence to the status quo, acceptance that 'it is what it is', has the potential to indicate that mediocre is sufficient and that fighting for what you believe is right or trying harder is not worth it.

Board quotas for women

The picture in the Middle East is mixed regarding quotas of any kind for women in leadership roles or committee and board membership. A 20% quota was introduced in Saudi Arabia for the Shura Council several years ago. Many countries in the region do not publish the figures of female board members. The UAE passed a law requiring all listed companies to have at least one woman board member by the end of 2020. In the same year, one-third of Dubai Financial Market companies had women board members. Elsewhere, the figures are not impressive. A 2018 State Street Global Advisory report found that of 170 listed companies across the GCC countries, 147 (85.6%) had no female board members.[20] In spite of these low figures, Reem (not her real name), an Emirati whose job is Head of Marketing, thought that board quotas, at least in the UAE, have had the most significant impact in creating opportunities for women and leadership in the past three years.

Representation of women on UK boards still has some way to go too. A five-year target was met by 2015 to have a minimum of 25% of board posts held by women. A further target was achieved in early 2020 for FTSE100 companies to have at least one-third of board positions being held by women. Whilst this might be seen as progress, these figures only relate to the UK's 100 largest companies. The study, published by The Hampton-Alexander Review, also found that there was a lack of women in senior roles in organisations and women accounted for just 15% of finance directors.[21] Incredibly, there are still senior women I have worked with who have been asked to serve tea at meetings or take notes. These kinds of biases about women's roles still exist.

Women could do more for themselves as well. I have spoken to many women who do not put themselves forward for board roles or to chair sub-committees on topics with which they are unfamiliar. They feel they have to learn more and be fully prepared before they apply. On the other hand, men do apply even though they know that sometimes they do not know the topic inside out, but they are often more courageous and prepared to take the risk of learning as they go.

Iceland has always encouraged women to sit on boards, and ensured equal opportunities in pay, mentoring and education. Norway was the first country in Europe to introduce quotas for women on boards in 2003. They reached the required 40% in seven years. The Nordic countries together have the highest number of women on boards.

Quotas can have a polarising effect. One argument says that if they are not in place, women will find it harder to achieve, and it will take longer for them to gain board positions. The other argument is that board members should be appointed on merit and bringing in women for the sake of numbers is no guarantee of competence. This has been a barrier for many women to step into leadership positions. Others have reached positions of seniority through their roles in family-owned companies. Sceptical observers may well consider that this is an easy route to seniority. In my experience, the women I have met in the Middle East who are working in family businesses are highly qualified, well educated, work hard, and many have travelled abroad for studies and to experience working life in a different country. Even in these family enterprises, they still have to prove their worth.

Government initiatives in the Middle East

Some Middle East governments have actively encouraged the development of women into more senior leadership roles, not just locally but internationally. All the women I spoke to for this book felt that there had been changes in the Middle East in the past three years since I carried out my previous research. This is certainly the case in the UAE. Maha Bin Hendi is Emirati and set up her own law firm in Dubai in 2017. She was very emphatic about the changes, *"Emirati women are now ambassadors, diplomats, ministers, members of the Federal National Council (FNC), CEOs of major companies, leaders, and pioneers in numerous fields and sectors."*

In 2006, the government in Dubai launched the Dubai Women Establishment. The aim was to support women to move into the workforce and help retention when they married and had children. Since then, there have been several more initiatives for women, including the launch of the Gender Balance Council in 2015. A year later, the Council launched a Gender Inequality Index. In 2020, there were nine women in the UAE Cabinet, up from eight in 2017. In other countries in the region, only Kuwait, Lebanon, Morocco, Tunisia, Algeria, Oman and Bahrain had women members of the Cabinet in 2020. In addition to female participation in the UAE Cabinet, the government issued a directive that at least half of the 40 seats on the FNC should be held by Emirati women.

Farah, an Emirati with her own architectural consultancy, saw these developments as having had a major influence on women seeking out more leadership roles in the UAE as well as having an international impact. She referred to Her Highness Sheikha Fatima bint Mubarak who was granted the Agent of Change Award by the United Nations – the UN entity for gender empowerment.

Women in senior roles are certainly driving women and leadership initiatives forward. There is no lack of government support either, and it seems to me that one of the main differences for women in the UAE compared with many other countries is that this government message is consistently reinforced. This has given women permission to pursue their ambitions at work and introduced an expectation that they can achieve their ambitions to be leaders in their organisations. It is not only that, said Lina Farajallah, a Consultant in People Development and Project Management who is half Ukrainian and half Palestinian and has lived in the UAE, "The *UAE government is increasing competition and economic globalisation, which in return forms more flexible, cooperative, holistic and modern organisations that are enhancing the UAE women's labour market position.*"

Even so, there is still a lag between what the UAE government is saying and what is actually happening in some companies in the Emirates. It is not entirely clear whether everyone is getting a sense of where the focus is. Hiba is Lebanese and has worked for a global company in the UAE. She was not sure whether the government initiatives had made a difference to opportunities for women overall. She did acknowledge that the appointment of HE Shamma Al Mazrui as Minister of Youth in 2016 was significant, more so because she was only 22 at the time. It is worth noting that in 2020 the minister still held the record for the youngest ministerial appointment anywhere in the world.

The barriers to progression and the gap between the high levels of education and declining positions at work is pause for thought. The UAE government has been very clear that the responsibility to change lies with the organisations themselves. As well as female cabinet ministers, there are some outstanding women at senior levels in organisations. However, progress has not been as rapid in some entities as in others. Not all companies have an explicit pathway for women to progress into leadership roles either.

Hamda Alshamali is Emirati and for two years has been Executive Director of Human Resources at a large insurance company which is locally owned and based in the Gulf. She said that in her organisation there was no clear road map for women and leadership and targets had not been set either. Companies should be investing in female leadership and supporting women's growth and development. There should be more belief in *"equality and fair opportunities regardless of your gender, colour, etc."*

Lubna Qassim, the Executive Vice President of Emirates NBD Bank, its General Counsel and Company Secretary, has expressed her frustration that changes are not happening quickly enough. In her view, CEOs, who are mainly men and the budget holders, have to sponsor these initiatives, but they do not know how to do it, particularly at senior level.[22]

Even though the government is supporting women, there was more that had to be done in Middle Eastern society, considered Natalia, a Ukrainian working in the UAE as a Sales Manager. *"The fact that the government of the UAE is supporting women in leadership does not have enough influence. There is a cultural factor which is playing a massive role in all Middle East countries. Women are still brought up like followers, but not like leaders."* By contrast, Sama, an Emirati special needs teacher, felt one noticeable change had been a shift in roles at home, *"The balance of roles between men and women in the household whereby they are contributing equally in house chores and childcare. Men in all aspects of life (father, brother, husband, manager) are encouraging women to build a career and pursue the things they like."*

In the wider region, there have been changes in Jordan as well, according to Randa, a Jordanian Project Manager. She said the difference to women's empowerment during the last three years had come about through access to social media, *"Social media platforms gave many women a voice and lots of exposure. Also, the paradigm shift in society that accepts women in multiple positions."* Linda Al Ali, a Jordanian Business Development Manager in a media company, felt that Queen Rania Al Abdullah of Jordan had created a positive drive for women in Jordan. *"Her Majesty... highlighted the importance of role models for Arab women, and also reaffirmed the significance of education in dispelling misconceptions about women's rights in Islam."* She also praised Queen Rania's involvement in the Women's Leadership Initiative which encourages women to get involved in global issues. She thought this was probably the most significant thing the Queen was doing.

There have been changes in Saudi Arabia too. Badia (not her real name) is a Saudi Arabian HR Director at a large government-owned investment fund. She thought the biggest impact had been the country's leadership and their encouragement and support for more women leaders. Thana (not her real name), also a Saudi Arabian national and Chief of Staff in her organisation agreed with Badia. She was pleased that more women were being appointed to senior roles and *"...new sectors are opening up for them."*

شُجَاعَة

CHAPTER 4

TAKING CARE OF YOURSELF FIRST

"Put your own oxygen mask on before helping other people with theirs." Anyone who has ever taken a flight will be familiar with this phrase in the safety briefing before take-off. It is a good motto to keep in mind all the time. I strongly advocate that anyone already in a leadership position or who wants to move into a more senior role has to manage their self-care and think about what their own mental and physical needs are if they are not doing it already. Being of service to others in a leadership role, at whatever level of the company, means starting with yourself first. Creating space for self-care in the form of leisure, fitness, diet, sleep and social time with family and friends means that you can be at your best at work in any capacity. Flourishing and growing as a leader works from inside out as well as outside in.

If the Covid-19 pandemic taught us anything, it highlighted the need for good mental health. Too often, leaders have focused their energies on others and not enough on themselves. Time to think is often cited by leaders as one of the greatest benefits of executive coaching. Leaders are usually in the thick of it most of the time, and the firefighting that goes with the position is exacerbated in crisis. Taking time out to think and reflect is an opportunity to check in with themselves and how they are feeling.

Self-preservation

Even if you are not yet in your desired role, it is never too early to start getting into the practice of remembering self-care. Many different approaches can be used to preserve your personal mental health or mental hygiene as well as your physical health. Those people who already have methods in place take part in activities which suit them best or those they have access to. Meditation and mindfulness are popular, but not everyone finds them easy or appealing. For you, it may be a welcome way of helping you to restore your energy. Other people like to exercise either inside or outside, depending on the temperature. Anywhere is suitable so long as it provides a place and space for you to have time to think and process what is happening not just at work but also in your personal life.

You may prefer team activities. Social contact might be quite important to you and being around others in a leisurely setting can restore your energy. Other people prefer time alone. For them, the best way to feel refreshed and restored is doing something quietly on their own. The key here is to allow yourself time to process, reflect and think.

Claim back your agenda at work

Too often we go to work and launch straight into the working day, which is punctuated by constant meetings, webinars, more meetings, calls, dealing with sudden events. Some of these are unavoidable, of course. The common practice in so many organisations of open calendars, in my view, is a major contributory factor to the pressures for all staff. It often means there are no gaps between meetings and no time for anyone to mentally leave one meeting and prepare for the next one. As soon as a meeting organiser sees a space, they put another meeting in without considering individual needs. If there is no mechanism to change this practice, think about the priority of these meetings: do you need to attend all of them? Some you may have to, but if not, can one of your team go in your place? It is an opportunity for them to be more visible and learn and develop.

When you create some space for yourself during the day, you can use this time to consider what went well the day before and what could have been different. You might have had a tricky conversation the day before. It is often better to let the brain subconsciously process what happened while you are sleeping. The old saying of 'sleeping on it' has some basis in science. It will probably give you a more objective perspective, as well as feeling more at ease with what happened. It does not just apply to conflict or a problem either. You may be looking for ideas or different ways to work on a project. Letting ideas emerge rather than forcing them results in a lot more creative thinking and can lead to more innovative solutions.

I have suggested this approach to many of my clients, especially those who are feeling overwhelmed with work and have lost a sense of structure in their day. It sometimes feels counterintuitive. If it seems hard to do this, imagine some of the benefits you might gain. For example, you could make notes at the end of each week about how you are feeling; think about the amount of work you got through, what went well, and what you learned about yourself. If it does not suit you to take a pause each morning before you start work, try clearing one afternoon a week to catch up with yourself.

I had one client in a global organisation who made herself unavailable for meetings at the end of the working week in the afternoon. Over time, she began to feel better organised, found more time to interact with existing colleagues and got to know people she had not met before. She also developed a more strategic view of her role and what she could add to the organisation which could be of real value. It made a positive difference to how she felt both physically and mentally and had a profound impact on her sense of wellbeing. She was creating better boundaries around what was important and what could wait. Being able to establish boundaries is a useful skill to have. It makes it clear to everyone how you work, and it also protects you from taking too much on.

Brain breaks

The executive 'thinking' part of the brain is situated in the pre-frontal cortex at the very front of your brain, behind your forehead in effect. This part of the brain uses up an enormous amount of energy, including taking glucose from other parts of the body to keep it going. It is where decisions are made, and it tires very easily.

Studies about learning for children suggest that information is usually only retained effectively if learning is carried out in 20-minute chunks. This applies to adults too. The idea is that people should adopt a daily pattern of rotating a short break after 20 minutes to walk around, have a drink and even something sweet to replace some of that glucose, then a further 20 minutes of work, another short break, another chunk of 20 minutes and then a longer break.

This process was famously developed into what is known as the 'Pomodoro Technique'® by the Italian Francesco Cirillo in the 1980s as a time-management tool. He named it Pomodoro after his kitchen timer, which was shaped like a tomato. There are several mobile phone applications which do similar things. Clearly, it is not always practical or possible to work in this way but finding some way of carving out space to pause is valuable.

Afternoons are a time when many people have an energy dip and crave sweet things. Taking a proper break for lunch, getting some fresh air if possible and eating helps to boost that glucose supply and prevents some fatigue. Even so, brain energy can plateau later in the day, and there is a higher risk of decisions being flawed. This is commonly referred to as decision fatigue. This applies as much to people who tend to be early risers as it does to people who go to bed late. The brain is freshest in the morning and that is the best time to make decisions. Research on recruitment shows there is a higher likelihood of making the right choice for the vacancy when these hiring decisions are made early in the day. If you are ever invited to an interview and are able to choose a time, always pick the morning![23]

Managing daily stress

One of the most important reasons for managing your time in these ways is to prevent complete overload. The gradual attrition of this sense of wellbeing, a feeling of loss of control can be damaging if it is not checked. Worry and anxiety overload the brain, and those healthy-state decisions become flawed, sometimes impetuous, irrational and problematic. The gatekeepers for the brain, the amygdala, situated in the limbic system, go on high alert. They are always 'on' which is mentally exhausting. These high levels of stress cause the brain to flood with cortisol and adrenaline. These are neurotransmitters which are triggered when the brain is under threat. This is all well and good when there is a fire. But the continual flood of these neurotransmitters which are released by stress is unhealthy and has nowhere to go. It disrupts sleep, can affect appetite and mood amongst other things, may cause panic and anxiety attacks, and if left can lead to burnout and exhaustion.

In 2019, LinkedIn commissioned a study with Censuswide on working patterns.[24] The survey was conducted in the

UAE and Saudi Arabia. Results showed that more than 65% of employed people felt overworked, and 45% of millennials in the UAE and 24% in Saudi Arabia did not use up all their holiday time. More than 1,000 people took part in the survey and were aged 18 or over, and self-identified as being in full-time, part-time or freelance employment. In the survey, many of the respondents expressed they had developed symptoms of burnout if there had been a gap of more than three months from their last holiday.

We can all deal with a certain amount of stress. Indeed, it is good for us and the brain. The manageable load is when we are coping with our daily life and everything is reasonably smooth, both at work and outside. Psychiatrist Dr Dan Siegel refers to this as our 'window of tolerance'.[25] Imagine a large window. This window represents our daily lives when stresses and strains are under control and part of our usual daily rhythm. Any tensions are usually balanced out, within the window, by the good things that are happening during each day. Any perceived threat is countered by the reward neurotransmitters, oxytocin and dopamine, which make us feel good and relaxed. This keeps our window of tolerance wide and gives us more scope and energy to deal with what is happening each day. However, when things run out of control and we start to feel overwhelmed and unable to keep up, the window shrinks, and we have reduced capacity to deal with stress. Continued stress at this level can make us impulsive, take unnecessary risks, be full of dread in a less than rational way, tearful or angry. Alternatively, when the overwhelm is so great, we can become flat and empty, disconnected, slow thinking and absent, even if we are in the room. People suffering in this way often fall into depression, and it can take a long time to recover. These effects may also be seen following trauma.

Mental health

People who reach these extreme points may not always recognise it. Even if they do, they may not be willing or prepared to acknowledge it. This is when the negative self-talk begins to creep in. They often feel they 'should' be able to cope and deal with anything that comes their way in their role. Added to this, there is often a stigma attached to anything to do with mental health.

Saudi Arabia was included in a survey about mental health conducted by Ipsos MORI and King's College, London in 2019.[26] Twenty-nine countries were invited to participate to find out what cultural differences there were in attitudes to mental health issues around the world. Of the people from Saudi Arabia who responded to the questionnaire, a quarter of them thought that increasing expenditure on mental health was a waste of money, even though 61% thought that mental and physical health were equally important. Nearly a third thought anyone with a history of mental illness should be excluded from public office.

If more people could be open about what is happening, it would become easier to discuss transparently. It may not be obvious to others. People suffering can get quite clever at hiding it. They keep going at work, and some even try to hide it at home. Although they do not want to be in this state, sympathy and understanding are not forthcoming. Unlike someone who has broken an arm or a leg and is in plaster, mental health is invisible. But it is also insidious when your mental health is not in a good state and can have damaging long-term effects.

Gradually men and women with household names are beginning to speak out publicly about their own experiences which is raising more awareness and is going some small way towards normalising mental health problems and reducing any stigma. It is a taboo subject in many parts of the world. The difficulty for men in being open about it may well be the hard-wiring they have that they are the copers, the fixers; they are in charge. Many women find it difficult to talk about as well. Feeling comfortable enough to be open about mental health problems is not gender-specific.

What is encouraging is that people in business are also speaking out. In 2011, Lloyds Banking Group in London appointed a new CEO, António Horta-Osório. Just a few months after he started, Horta-Osório took a leave of absence for two months. He spoke openly about the overload of the new job and that he had experienced a period of five days with no sleep. In effect, his brain was fuzzy, but he struggled on until the fatigue overwhelmed him, and he suffered a physical collapse. At that time, very few high profile figures spoke openly in this way, and he was recognised for his courage in doing so. Fortunately, he recovered well, remained healthy and spent a further ten years as CEO before announcing he would be stepping down in 2021.

The irony is that if an employee was in this position, and their manager was aware, they would probably be sympathetic and compassionate. As with self-care, compassion begins with self-compassion. You cannot be truly compassionate towards those you lead if you are not being compassionate with yourself as well.

Much as you may feel uncomfortable about it, you still need to fight for what you believe is right. It will not just come to you. The desire and wish that the existing system in your particular organisation means that recognition, equal pay, appropriate promotion and the rest will just happen is misguided. Part of the process is for you to be seen to care about all these things, be prepared to put your stake in the ground for what you believe you can do. This means negotiating, in a calm and respectful way, about what you want. It may be about your salary; it may be about your next promotion. It will mean having conversations with those who can influence the decisions, playing politics to an extent if you have to, provided it is congruent and consistent with your beliefs.

Something to guard against is letting any sense of injustice or lack of fairness overwhelm your thinking. This is another negative trigger for the brain. If you do start to feel this way, it can be dispiriting and demotivating and eventually work output will suffer. It might affect your health too. If you are not enjoying your work, you will probably not be feeling too good either, both emotionally and physically. Make sure that if you are negotiating, you choose a moment and a time when you are feeling positive.

You have to speak up for you. This is very different from a sense of entitlement. Entitlement is when people think they have a right to promotion and opportunities without adding effort to the work they are currently doing. Consider this: if you do not speak out about what you would like, if you do not make a stand for what you believe in, how will others who have influence even know what it is you stand for? If there is a job vacancy in a more senior or different role from the one you are doing, why not apply for it? If nothing else, it will show that you are interested in developing your career, that you have a commitment to the company and that you want to grow and learn.

I think that very little of this is possible without the sense of self-care that it is so important to develop as you strive towards your leadership goal. If you feel good, if your energy levels are where they should be and you feel healthy, that is the time when you can showcase your best self. Self-care includes thinking about what your priorities are, what your cultural values are, your purpose and what is important in your life and how you want to live it. Putting your healthiest self at the centre of your dreams and ambitions for your working life and your aspirations towards leadership is most definitely the first step towards achieving your goals for yourself.

شُجَاعَة

CHAPTER 5

MAKING A DIFFERENCE IN THE WORLD

You may well have one or several people in your life who you admire. These people might inspire you and help you to keep on track with your own aspirations, your high dreams now and your dreams from childhood and what you would like to achieve as an adult. It can be highly motivating to see people in public life achieving the kind of success you would like to have or finding recognition and successes in spite of a difficult start in life. Even if you have never met them, watching how their careers have developed can feel enabling, "If she/he can do it, so can I!" They can come from any walk of life; they might be someone from your family or social group and are not gender-specific either. It might be the best teacher you had in school, a politician, actor, author, leader of a company or could even be a grandparent or parent.

The point is that thinking about someone in this way, assessing how they have managed hardships and their achievements regardless of their position can give you the courage to keep going when things get tough. If this is something that you have never thought about, it might be worth thinking about it now. It might be someone you know very well, but even if it is someone you are never likely to meet, learn something about how they coped with disappointments, success and in particular, what they have learned about themselves.

In the context of organisational leadership, successful leaders may not necessarily be perceived as role models, but they do inspire their people. Who inspires you, and who would you like to inspire? These leaders are highly regarded and respected in their organisations by their colleagues, teams and bosses. It seems to me that it is this inspirational characteristic which good leaders of organisations have, even if they are sometimes difficult to deal with. These are the servant-leaders, the ones who create the environment and culture which generates trust and enables their people to flourish. They care about their people. These are the kind of people who make a difference in the world of work. How do you want to make a difference in the world?

The stereotypes associated with women

In the United States, 71% of HR-related roles were held by women according to a 2019 American HR Careers Report.[27] Business departments connected with people management in organisations with names such as Human Resources, People Development or Personnel are often considered to be female-dominated, and consequently, men might be put off from choosing this direction in their careers.

It is tempting to argue that women have naturally leaned towards those kinds of roles because it is about caring and looking after people. We already know that women are better at negotiating for their teams than they are for themselves. Women do care about people and want to do the best for them. Men care about people too. Nevertheless, it is interesting to consider what happens as girls and boys go through childhood and then into adulthood. As small children, there is still a big distinction in many cultures about the differences between girls and boys. In Arab culture, this is well defined. Women are often treated as fragile, not able to think for themselves and incapable of making decisions. They are brought up to obey men. The language used to describe boys and girls is different too. There can be a reaction when women start working and see that the men they work with are getting more favourable treatment, or their opinions and decisions are accepted, whereas women's opinions and decisions are often criticised or disregarded.

The distinctions in the use of language in performance appraisals or even feedback conversations vary too. A

classic example is when men have been described as
assertive or forthright, and women have been described as
bossy or aggressive. Men sometimes describe women this
way if they are trying to make a point in meetings.

This happened to a client of mine who was working in
a MENA country outside the GCC. She came to me for
coaching to help increase her confidence. She was the
only woman in a team of six people and was experiencing
frequent sidelining at meetings, not being invited to give
her opinions and being interrupted or even cut off when
she did say anything. The most upsetting event was a
project that they were working on as a team. She had
done much of the work for it and when it was presented
to the manager, he complimented the team on their work,
highlighting particular points which had all been part of
her contribution. Her colleagues claimed the credit and no
one referred to her input. This made her feel invisible and
had resulted in her becoming increasingly demotivated
and undermined.

We started by exploring ways of managing her internal
feelings and how she might access good things to do outside
work that would start to give her more positive things to
think about rather than spending all her time dwelling
on work. We also discussed how she could challenge the
situation herself, rather than complaining to her manager.
She realised that she was struggling all the time internally
against her upbringing in quite a traditional household
with several brothers. At home, she did not have much
time to spend on doing things for herself because she was
expected to be available all the time for the family. This
pattern was repeating itself at work.

During the coaching, I encouraged her to make notes about what was going well and to keep adding to it every day. This would remind her of her strengths. The coaching supported her to develop her own plan to confront the situation in a respectful way with the team. She started to be firmer when she had a point to make, and eventually she was able to give the team direct feedback about the effect their behaviour had been having on her. Rather than singling out anyone in particular, she framed the conversation in terms of the benefit it would bring to all of them as a team, and the organisation, if they worked in a more inclusive and collaborative way. This meant it did not come across as an ambush. Her colleagues had not realised what they were doing and committed to changing their attitude towards her and other female colleagues. At the end of our coaching contract, the team were working well together, and my client found going to work a real pleasure again. Most important though, she was feeling much better in herself. Her confidence had grown and she was positive about the future.

Hiba felt male attitudes like this were a challenge across the region, and changes needed to start at home. *"When mothers ask their boys and girls to make their beds, this is where change becomes effective and effortless. In the Middle East, men are born entitled. Women are expected to exert double the effort to get equal status. When I got married, I made it a big fuss not to leave the dining table to get salt. If my husband wanted salt, he could go and get it."* She called this her *"small revolution... we need to build courage, accept breaking moulds, and be unapologetically oneself, without the need to fit in."* If women demonstrated this to their children, and it was combined with a good education and continuous learning, they would grow into men and women *"equipped to compete in leadership opportunities irrespective of their gender."*

Conscious and unconscious bias

There is still automatic categorising in many organisations, in spite of all the moves towards gender equality. Unconscious bias and conscious bias towards women still persist in many cultures, not just in the Middle East. We all have biases of one kind or another, and it is important to be aware of our own as well as drawing attention to examples of it in action.

Unconscious bias develops through our earliest influences when we begin the process of social learning through facial recognition in infancy. This becomes hard-wired, and this facial information becomes our way of processing social information. This continues into adulthood without us realising it. Typical influences will come from a wide range of experiences, including parents, family, school, religion, gender and culture.

Economist and Psychologist Dr Daniel Kahneman calls this part of our brain System 1 thinking. He says we humans use 90% of our cognition with this part of the brain.[28] It is automatic, unconscious and quick. Much of it is nuanced and comes through small behaviours such as mannerisms, body language, eye contact and tone of voice. As the human brain develops into adulthood, this way of social processing begins to lay down neural pathways, and it becomes hard-wired and fixed. The combination of all these influences creates the unique lens that each of us has when we try to make sense of the world. In cultures and societies like MENA, social learning has rested heavily on the belief systems regarding the role of men and their superiority over women.

The best way to overcome unconscious bias is to raise awareness of it and then manage it. This can be done by learning which unconscious biases you have and consciously reflecting on how they show up in your interactions. According to Kahneman, this means using the remaining 10% of your thinking, which he refers to as System 2 thinking. This is when we do our critical thinking. It is conscious, precise and deliberate.

An experiment to find out why there was a lack of gender diversity in national orchestras in the United States led to some significant understanding of the impact of unconscious bias when it comes to selection. In 1970, fewer than 6% of the players in the five highest ranked orchestras were women. They wondered if their selections might be based on some kind of unconscious bias against women candidates and devised a way to test the theory. Instead of potential candidates being visible, they were asked to play their instruments behind a closed curtain and without shoes. Unconsciously, the interview panel (usually all men) were identifying women from the sound of their shoes. Without realising it, their unconscious biases in favour of men being better players were affecting their choice of candidate. They were not listening to how well candidates played their instruments or judging them on their musical ability. Their biases were making the decisions for them. Blind auditions were systematically introduced for orchestra selection, and by 1993 the number of women players had trebled. In 2020, women represented 50% of the New York Philharmonic and a third of the Boston Symphony Orchestra.[29]

Men can also raise awareness of unconscious bias against women. At the 2016 Olympics, tennis champion Andy Murray was praised in an interview with a male sports reporter for being the first person in tennis to win two gold medals. Murray immediately pointed out that both champion tennis players Serena Williams and Venus Williams had won four gold medals each. Serena later praised him for his quick response in calling out the interviewer's unconscious bias. He had automatically thought that it was only possible for a male tennis player to have achieved this success.

Queen Bees

It is the case that some women, once they achieve positions of leadership, do little to help support other women coming up the ladder behind them and are completely task-focused. Sometimes referred to as 'Queen Bees', these women create a coterie of men around them who are seen by many to be there because they are in awe of the Queen Bee and do not challenge her. It is worth noting that there is not an equivalent male term for this kind of leadership. Margaret Thatcher was considered to be a strong Queen Bee when she was Prime Minister of the United Kingdom between 1979 and 1990. Although she had impact, it did not include much support for the development of women.

Thatcher surrounded herself with some extremely clever and wise politicians, nearly all men, many of whom were good people in their own right, but very few were prepared to challenge her decision making. Those that did were often sacked from her Cabinet. At times it appeared that she wanted to be seen as 'one of the boys'. Leaders like this often have a swift descent from the top. Cocooned in her own power, Thatcher failed to see any signs of discontent around her and stopped listening to close advisors trying to warn her that she was losing support as the leader within her government. By the time she sacked her Chancellor of the Exchequer whom she had disliked intensely, it was already too late, and his legendary and revengeful resignation speech eventually triggered a challenge to her leadership which she lost.

Queen Bees can be critical of other women on the grounds of emotionality or that they have not tried hard enough or are not committed enough to go for leadership positions. One of the reasons they do not like to have women in their teams is because, underneath the seemingly tough exterior, they see women as a threat to their position. They are worried they will be exposed and shown not to have all the skills they need to lead. Hana Al-Syead thought that women tended to misinterpret how they can be part of the problem. They tried hard to fit into a male-designed work culture, overlooking the fact that it was not designed with them in mind. Arab women do not always help themselves in this kind of scenario.

I carried out group facilitation with an all-female team at a large locally owned company in the Gulf which required quite a bit of mediation as well as coaching. All five of the team had fallen out and were either arguing, ignoring each other, or being hypercritical. Behaviours were out of control, and the manager seemed to be angry with someone in the team all the time. This had a ripple effect throughout the department, and the behaviour validated many of their male colleagues' stereotypical views that women should not be working because they are too emotional, not very clever and cannot cope with pressure because they are too fragile. Although it took this unhappy team a while to recover from all the disagreements they had been having, they did eventually find a way of working together.

What really helped them move forward was the creation of a team contract. They each contributed ideas, and together we pulled out the key elements that they felt should be in the contract. These included topics like meeting deadlines, sharing ideas, appreciating everyone's contribution, allowing equal time for each team member to speak during meetings and be listened to, as well as behaving respectfully towards each other. They all signed the document. Doing this meant that each team member, including the manager, could be held accountable by everyone if any parts of the contract were not being met. Some months later, I heard that some other teams had adopted a similar approach to how they would like to work together.

In conversation with some of the women I have met in the years I have been working in the Middle East, I have come across several who do not want to have a female manager because of this kind of volatility. They prefer to have male managers because they at least know what they are dealing with and understand the dynamics and Arab male psyche so well. Hana Al-Syead put it this way, *"Women tend to compete by crushing other women. Men won't necessarily choose to crush women; they'll simply try to outwin them."* This can happen globally, not just in the Middle East.

Task-focused or people-focused?

I challenge the assumption that women can either be task-focused or people-focused but not both. They can be both, and there are plenty of men who can be both as well. What is your understanding of being task-focused or people-focused? In organisations, you will know people who want to get the job done. Their focus is on objectives, getting projects finished and delivered on time. Their priority centres on the outcomes and how they will benefit the organisation. Systematic in approach, they are likely to concentrate on the business case for completion of objectives. Consideration of people's feelings comes second in the priority list. On the other hand, those who are more people-focused tend to work the other way round. They think about the impact on people first, consider their needs and feelings and what needs to be taken into account in order to complete objectives. Are you more people-focused or task-focused, or either depending on the situation?

As an example, if you had to cut your department from ten people to seven, how would you make the choice of who to lose? Would you look logically at the qualities of each person and assess what they contribute to the company in terms of their value to the organisation? Or would you find it hard to be that systematic because you could not avoid thinking about someone who might be the only earner in their family, or have big medical bills to pay for a family member? What is important to understand about these two preferences is that everyone can be both task-focused and people-focused. Neither of these preferences is right or wrong. The trick is being able to blend when necessary or know which kind of focus is most appropriate in a given moment. This is how you can make a difference.

Women leaders during the 2020 pandemic

The Prime Minister of New Zealand, Jacinda Ardern, has proved that women can be both people- and task-focused. Since Ardern became New Zealand's premier in 2017, her small country of just 5 million people has been hit by a series of national events which have brought the country under a global spotlight. There have been earthquakes, mass shootings, and then the Coronavirus pandemic. A quote from an interview she gave to the *New York Times* in 2018[30] was repeated several times on social media in 2020 because of her successful handling of the pandemic in New Zealand, *"One of the criticisms I've faced over the years is that I'm not aggressive enough or assertive enough or maybe somehow, because I'm empathetic, it means I'm weak. I totally rebel against that. I refuse to believe that you cannot be both compassionate and strong."*

When the 2020 pandemic first arrived, nations with female leaders fared much better than those with male leaders in containing the virus. As well as New Zealand, some of the countries with female leaders included Germany, Taiwan and Denmark. What were the qualities they had in common that stood out? At the time that the crisis became a pandemic, very few countries were being led by women. Nevertheless, these countries successfully halted the spread well before other nations. A research study conducted in 2020 revealed that some of the reasons behind this were to do with risk aversion.[31] These female leaders valued the loss of life as greater than risks to the national economy. In addition, they communicated openly and honestly about the dangers; they were decisive and demonstrated empathy with people's situations. They showed that they could blend both task-focus and people-focus successfully and appropriately to lead their nations and their people through the crisis.

I would suggest that all these women have also had to fight quite hard to get to where they are now. They may also have had an upbringing which encouraged them to feel they could achieve anything they wanted regardless of their gender, or they may have had an upbringing which has made them determined to succeed or make the world better, make their country better. They have had to be fierce. They have also had to be bold.

My sense is that the women I have worked with in the Middle East have a proud fierceness too. Even though some of the obstacles they are facing are tightly bound and woven by their culture, they hear the call. Gradually they are claiming their rightful place at work and making a difference in the world.

شُجَاعَة

CHAPTER 6

YOU CAN HAVE IMPACT BY BEING BOLD

What does making your mark in the world of work mean? How does anyone make their mark? Maybe a better approach is to look at what needs to happen so that you are noticed, are visible and that your contribution to an organisation is valued and appreciated.

I have become aware over time that the women from the Middle East who I know, and those who I have worked with, have one thing in common if they have a strong desire to move into leadership roles or are already there. They have not waited for someone to come and ask them, they have pushed for promotion and stated their ambitions and intentions. In this culture where it is still very much a man's world, this is hard to do. Nevertheless, unless you are prepared to step up and claim what is yours, it is not going to happen in the way you might like it to, or as quickly as you would like it to. Sama advised women to help themselves more by going beyond their job description to take on bigger challenges at work and identify roles they were interested in. This would mean that senior management would *"see their potential first-hand"*.

Showing that initiative may be the only thing standing in your way. Instead of assuming that your request will probably be turned down, so there is no point in asking, assume that it will not be turned down. If it is, find out why and do not let that put you off. You might have to make a case for it, and in your own organisation you will know what the benefits could be, not just to you but also to the company in terms of return on investment. If you want to be a leader, you need to learn more about it and more about the world of work.

Expand your leadership learning

One way to build your knowledge about leadership is to read about it and hear examples of other women's experiences, according to Hiba. She also thought it was important not to be risk-averse. *"Take risks, even when it is VERY uncomfortable. If you are hard-working and persistent, it will eventually pay off."* Hiba recommended joining or building a professional network outside work. It was an effective way to gain skills and learn about other kinds of business.

In addition to networking, Maha Bin Hendi advised women to ask for coaching and mentoring. *"I also believe in mingling with experts and intellects that could help improve their understanding and skills in developing their leadership roles."* Attending workshops was *"vital"* according to Maha. Advancement was all about setting appropriate targets for short- and long-term career success. *"Women have to believe in themselves first and know what they want."*

Women who wanted to learn more about leadership should be thinking from a wider perspective, said Farah. *"Women should be more daring in gaining knowledge in politics, immerse themselves deeper into its context, and boldly take the lead… whatever is necessary… with confidence that women are born to be leaders too."* This would also require *"moral support from the government as a sign of recognition and permission that it is timely to train women in all these aspects."*

It is already evident that women are better at negotiating for others than they are for themselves. Women do not want to feel they are being demanding. But it is worth considering that if a male colleague felt he wanted to progress and that there were tools and training he would find useful to help him, he would probably ask for them. Women need to do the same.

The main thing to keep in mind is that anything you aim to do developmentally is not to make you the same as everyone else. This is not about you becoming a mini-me version of some of your male colleagues. This is about you developing your skills to put you on an equal footing with your colleagues, whatever their gender. This is about you, the person, first and foremost.

In the culture of the Middle East, it is not always easy, particularly when your boss or the senior team is highly likely to be all-male, to push for your personal career development. Women in some of the region's countries do have a lot more freedom to express their career aspirations and go for what they dream of than in others. Traditional Arab culture is extremely respectful of parents, grandparents and more senior relations. Some of these more traditional families may be uncomfortable that their daughters are working, especially if they are mixing with men at work. Not only that, some women are keen to work to use their brains and feel some autonomy as well as earn some extra money.

In contrast, I know of incidents when husbands have been unhappy about their wife's promotion because it might mean longer hours and less availability for the wife to be involved in childcare and preparing the evening meal. The husbands have insisted that the promotion should not happen. Intimidated by their husbands, these women often do not speak up for themselves – quite unlike the confident behaviour they show to their work colleagues during the working day. They acquiesce, preferring to keep the peace and perhaps fearful of what life will be like at home if they do not. Even highly educated women choose their battles too. Their innate understanding of their own culture means they can deftly pick their way through social norms.

It is your choice

A further point to consider is company 'fit'. The organisational expert Jim Collins calls this, "getting the right people on the bus and the wrong people off the bus."[32] People themselves need to assess whether they are on the wrong bus to start with. It might happen after a while if the culture where they are working is no longer congruent with their personal values and the values of the company that employs them. Are you on the right bus?

Her Highness Dr Basma Al Said is a clinical psychologist in Oman. She set up the first women's clinic in Oman dealing with mental health and wellness. HH Basma says it took persistence and determination to make it work. *"Women need to take responsibility,"* she said unequivocally. *"Change starts with you. You have a choice..."*[33] Alia Al Nabooda, a board member at Khalifa Juma Al Nabooda Group and an Emirati, agreed with speaking out. *"Women need to be their own advocates and prove to the world that we are more than capable of doing any job."*

Nowadays, more women are setting up home on their own. They might need to negotiate with their family. They are also prepared to play a long game to get what they want. Knowing that you have some degree of self-sufficiency and can manage to live alone also helps to build confidence. It may also mean a shorter journey to work. Not having to make a long journey home means a fresher mind, more energy for important conversations which focus on your own career plans like seeking out training opportunities. Framing a request like this in terms of the benefit it can bring the organisation is often the best approach.

There may be opportunities to learn about teamwork, developing soft skills, or learning how to be a manager. Find out about impact surveys. Many of them show that this initial investment has great long-term gains, not just for you but also the organisation.

As far as Lina Farajallah was concerned, women deserved to become leaders and needed to trust their capabilities more. *"In the Middle East women are brought up believing that they are born to follow men, obey men, always go back to a father or brother or husband for permission, therefore taking them out of their comfort zone of finding someone to decide for them is not easy. This is why some women don't really mind having a male boss to decide and take responsibility."* Lina was clear about how much women should take responsibility for themselves and the impact this would have. *"By taking responsibility for their future they can teach future generations to depend on themselves and build the future they aspire to."*

In the face of resistance, if you are one of the women who feels that you are stuck in the 'squeezed middle' in your organisation, you may be wondering what you can actually do to push for change. What tools and support might help to make a difference? There are ways that you can make some small incremental changes. One way is to seek out female mentors in other organisations at senior level, where you might have the opportunity to get business advice that is unavailable in your own organisations.

What is mentoring?

The idea of a mentor is a trusted guide, someone who has already been in a similar position in the organisation or a different one, so can discuss at a granular level what they experienced and how they managed it. At a higher level, they will also have a more strategic view of the direction of a given organisation, may even know some of the key players, provide suggestions about managing difficult people and specifically managing upwards.

Some mentors might expect to be paid, but this tends to happen when someone is looking specifically for a business mentor who can advise on developing a business, such as a turnaround or new venture or even a startup. Many people choose to have a mentor from their own organisation. This might be fine if it is a big organisation with several divisions, and the mentor is far removed from the immediate environment the mentee is working in.

Be sure about the relationship this person might have with your manager. You need to feel that your mentor will be discreet. Some bosses are not comfortable with someone in their team having a mentor. They may see it as a threat. You will need to decide if you want your boss to know that you are being mentored. There is a risk that if you do not tell them, they may find out anyway and react badly. I also do not think it should be your boss. There are too many potential conflicts of interest and possible hidden agendas.

Mentoring from a previous boss, someone who knows you already, can be very effective. If you are aspiring towards a senior role, it may not be easy to be mentored by a man. To guard against a possible 'Queen Bee' situation, look around at some of the women who have achieved senior roles in a different company. Approach one or two and see if they would be willing to meet with you to discuss mentoring. In my experience, very few people will decline a request, especially women. After all, they have probably had similar experiences that you are having currently; they can talk to you in a more detailed way about how they went about planning their careers.

Above all, the person you choose needs to be someone you can trust. Your conversations with your mentor should be confidential and not be shared with anyone unless you give permission. Choose someone with good contacts and an excellent network too, especially if you want to broaden your career and move up or move company.

If you are being mentored by someone from outside your company, they can help you to learn about other organisations and how these organisations might be structured that might be different from yours. Be clear what you want from your mentor. It might be to help you understand your company better. Equally, it could be an opportunity for you to plan a career path and give you clarity about what you need to do to move into a leadership role. It could simply be a way for you to learn more about business, or the specific business you are in or the one you would like to move into.

This is why a mentor who has had wider experience may provide a better learning opportunity than someone who has stayed in one company for a long time, even if they have had several different roles. Whoever you choose, it should be someone who you feel has your best interests in mind and will help to develop your knowledge and increase your impact.

What is coaching?

As with mentoring, coaching is about asking good questions. A big difference is that unlike mentoring, coaching is not advisory. Coaches may make suggestions, but they will not tell you what to do. They serve as an equal thinking partner, their listening and questioning opens up their client's mind to looking at possibilities, coming up with their own solutions about their personal development, problem-solving, how to deal with poor performance, learning new skills, managing up as well as managing down and any hot topics that may be happening at the time.

Coaching is a contract, and the conversations are confidential. The aim of the coach is to create a safe environment for you to be able to reflect deeply on your coaching topic, understand what you wish for or need differently, and help you to draw out some next steps in the process. The agenda is the client's own. The way I see it, my client has a map of where they want to go. As their coach, I may have a compass and a torch to guide them, but the route and the destination are the client's own choice. This might be to do with behaviours, developing skills, understanding your manager or team better, as well as gaining some insights about yourself.

In between each coaching session, you would experiment and practise some of the actions that had been discussed and report back on how these are going. The important thing to keep in mind is that, as with learning a sport or a language, changing behaviours takes time, and the more you practise, the easier it will get.

Coaching can also support someone newly into a job or someone who is aiming to move into a higher position, such as their first leadership role. Coaches usually have a range of tools and models they use which can help their clients, as well as tips for them to take away.

Shujaa'ah

The question posed at the beginning of this chapter was about how anyone makes their mark. It is all very well to state that you can have impact by being bold. It depends, of course, on your definition of being bold. In Arabic, the feminine version of the word for bold is *shujaa'ah*. In the context of what is being written about here, boldness equates to being courageous, brave, undaunted and positive. Being bold means pushing boundaries, improving yourself and getting to know your abilities and becoming self-aware.

If you think about a time you feel you have shown courage, consider what transpired, what was the outcome and impact when you demonstrated courageousness. That courage might be something you did that you planned. It could also be a moment when you seized an opportunity that came your way because your instinct told you that you should. You may not have had much time to think about it, but you did it anyway. It could be that you had an opportunity to change your job, even your company.

Sometimes these opportunities come up at the wrong time. You may have had to decide quite quickly should you take the job or stay where you are. That kind of decision means being bold. It means taking the decision based on your best interests. You might even have used the opportunity of a job offer to go to your manager, explain the situation and get a sense of whether it would be a loss to your present company if you moved on. You might even be able to negotiate a pay rise, but if you do not ask for it, it is unlikely to happen. Women need to take responsibility for their own career progression.

Natalia gave some context as to why women may be reluctant to put themselves forward, *"Middle East culture is always trying to protect women. That's why women are used to relying on someone (father, brother or husband). They should have the opportunity to make mistakes and be responsible for it, learn how to handle life challenges without asking for permission. Only in this case will we be mentally ready to take the responsibility and be able to lead."*

Visibility

In my early career as a journalist in London, I was encouraged to apply for a promotion within the international television news company where I worked. It was quite a step up from my existing job, and I was not sure if I had the capability for it. The first of two interviews was with a panel of five men, all of whom I knew already. As I left the interview, one of them followed me out of the room. He and I had worked together a few years previously when he had been my boss. He told me that he had not realised what I had been doing since we worked together; he was surprised and had assumed I was still doing the same job all that time later.

This was a big lesson. I had not appreciated until then how important visibility is if you want to have an impact. I was offered the role, and I knew that what had made the difference was my determination not just to show the panel I was the best person for the position, but also the promise I made to myself to ensure that no one else would ever have so little idea of what I actually did in my job. If people do not know what you do at work, it might mean they do not know you either. If there is a job opening coming up that might be the perfect job for you, unless you step out of the shadows, no one will know you are even interested.

There are other ways to get visibility. For instance, think about the definition of your role in your organisation. If you look at the job specification of what you do and what your remit is, there might be areas around your job where you have an opportunity to take initiatives that connect into what you do. These initiatives can often be found by looking at what is **not** being done, rather than what is. This is not about doing a power grab. It is about raising your profile, adding something extra in however small a way so that you get seen for what you do and your contribution to the company. Randa thought this was something important for women to consider. She felt that women should do their best in their jobs and would get noticed by showing their growth and learning.

This is what being bold is. It means investing time looking at your own role and making it more efficient. Even by putting one or two small processes in place, you can make an impact, which not only benefits you and your team but also the organisation. You have a choice, but all this starts with you.

Finding your high dreams for leadership

According to the women I spoke to, the road map for women's leadership progression is far from clear in some companies, ranging from either non-existent to vague, or with no clear targets. In others, it is very clear, but this is attributed to the fact that these companies are MNCs, so the gender balance is much better. There seemed to be a significant difference in support for women where there was diversity at senior level. If this is not happening, Thana thought that women should learn to speak up, be assertive and change their mindset. She said organisations in Saudi Arabia need to give women more empowerment and have more women in managerial roles. Badia did not think the progression route was clear for men or women, *"It depends on network more than anything else… which men will win eventually as the bonds are tighter."* Badia referred to them as *"the wolf pack"*. She said it was important for women to be true to themselves but also not be overbearing towards others, and this had worked for her.

Imagine your highest dreams. If anything was possible, what would those high dreams be? Imagine saying to yourself, "What if..." rather than, "It's too hard" or, "I can't". Imagine how you would feel if you could reach your ambition to be a leader. Well, the good news is that you can get there. It all depends on your choices about what you want to do about it.

To help you consider those high dreams, it might be helpful to reflect back on how far you have travelled to this point now, wherever you are in your life and your job. Consider what your dreams and aspirations were as you moved through your education. There might have been a special teacher who really inspired you to believe in yourself. You may have had a high dream about the kind of career you wanted to have. It is also possible that you were not sure about whether you actually wanted a career and that what you really wanted to do was meet someone who you could share a happy and fulfilled life with and create a family.

Your family focus might have been just on your education and what you were learning. For you, the main thing was school, college, university and getting qualifications. Marriage was of secondary importance in your family's perspective. Your attitude to your education may have been energetic, and you were actively encouraged by your family to be fully committed to your studies. In your family, you might have been in the first generation to even get a full education and go on to university. This may have created a sense of obligation in you, that you should aim high and achieve the best you could to honour the support you were getting from your family. It is also possible that if you felt like this it might have given you a great drive to succeed and be first in class and a high achiever.

Then you had the decision to make about the kind of further education you wished to follow. This could have been one of those crunch points in your family discussions about the future. A university education definitely, but only if it was law or medicine. I have met women who wanted to be engineers. For some, it was quite a fight to get family agreement, and sometimes someone from the wider family would step in and support them. This was often an older relative who encouraged the parents to accept that times are changing and that these kinds of jobs – the ones that were traditionally 'male' – are now being carried out by women too. Sometimes a mother resisted these career choices out of concern that her daughter would not be seen to be eligible for marriage and that a potential husband would not want an educated wife who might be a challenge to him. I have also met women who accepted that the only way they could get support for a university education was to agree to either law or medicine and then change their minds further down the line and switch to something else.

There is also the question about going abroad to study. In some families, it is not acceptable for a young woman to travel alone and live away from her family in a foreign country. I met one young woman whose family agreed she could travel provided her mother went with her and lived with her while she attended university in her chosen country. The woman in question did not object to this at all, and she completed her studies successfully, enjoyed student life, and her mother also benefited from the experience.

Continuing these reflections about how you got to where you are now, you will have made some career choices when you completed your studies. Once you did that and started applying for jobs, think about whether it was your choice alone to take that first job opportunity. You may have been guided towards a career path by family and felt that you should choose a role that they approved of. As you revisit this time in your career, remember the energy and the excitement you felt as you stepped into the world of work. Remind yourself of the aspirations you had at that time and what has happened in the intervening period while you have been working. There will have been supporters and possibly detractors too as you worked your way into your current role, whether it is still the same organisation or a different one now.

Your legacy

When you look back at the learning you have achieved and the skills you have developed, it is worth asking yourself what you would like to have known then about working that you know now. The self-awareness you have developed and your skill set will probably have been learned in part from those around you but also the personal learning that you have accumulated along the way. Consider how you absorbed your learning: was it organic absorption or through active personal development opportunities? It might have been a mix of both or you could just have learned on the job. However you have accumulated your wider knowledge about working, how you are at work now is what matters, and how you are modelling these behaviours and skill sets that you have developed, so that others may be influenced by how you show up in the world.

A good question to ask yourself is what kind of legacy you would like to leave behind when you move into a different job or role or move organisations. What do you want people to say about you? Did you add value to their lives which benefited not only them but also the organisation? What did people feel when they interacted with you? Were you visible to them, and did you make them feel they were visible to you too? If you think about some of the people you worked with before now who have moved on to other companies, in all likelihood your memories will revolve around what they were like to work with and be with, not that they implemented some big shiny strategy or organised the office move to a different location. If you capture all these reflections and think about where your career is going next and what you want to achieve, you will realise that you already have most of the tools and skills to get you there.

Stretch your mindset

The only thing that might be holding you back from reaching higher is your own mindset about what you can achieve. Ask yourself about what kind of mindset you have. Is it a growth mindset or a fixed mindset? Dr Carol Dweck, a psychologist at Stanford University in California, first introduced this theory about mindset after many years of research.[34] She found that a sense of success is not just based on talent and ability but also on how successful people think about these two attributes. Her theory is that people generally have either a fixed or a growth mindset. Someone with a fixed mindset tends towards thinking that their personal abilities, capabilities and intelligence stay as they are and do not change. It is as if they are thinking,

'I've arrived, and I don't need to do any more'. They reach a particular level and stay there.

On the other hand, someone with a growth mindset understands that talents and capabilities can get even better with effort and persistence. Their attitude is more about 'I have got this far, but there is more I can learn and do'. These are the people with the most success. Dweck also draws attention to the risk of what she calls a 'false' growth mindset, meaning that you think you have it when actually you do not, or you have not fully grasped what a growth mindset means.

Think about your own mindset and be honest about it. Is it fixed, or do you want to grow? This is why developing your self-awareness is so important. Your aspirations to move into a senior leadership role will require commitment, perseverance, willingness to take risks, learning from your mistakes and not giving up when things do not go well. This is all part of having that growth mindset. You can choose which kind of mindset you like. But you may not get very far towards your leadership aspirations if you are not prepared to work hard for it, and it will take a lot of personal energy.

Being your best self

Something that will certainly contribute towards improving your energy is reflecting back on the chapter about self-care. It will always be important to acknowledge and meet your own physical and mental needs. Remind yourself that as much as the people around you deserve compassion and understanding, especially if times are tough, so do you. The fact is that you bring your whole self to work every day, however much you might like to think that you can compartmentalise different parts of your life.

For you to be your best self, all parts of your life need to be in flow and congruent. Your comfort in yourself follows on from this and ripples out into work and personal life. If one of the pillars of your life – and they are different for everyone – is not level with the other pillars, it causes imbalance. It is like a four-legged table. If one leg starts to wobble, it eventually affects the whole table. You can hide this lack of equilibrium for a while, but eventually it will leak out. Trying to be congruent, being something you are not, is a difficult position to maintain long term. The act of hiding is not good for your mental health either. Leadership is all about being the real you.

Now you have reviewed how you began your career, reminded yourself of the energy you had back then and where you are now, what are the feelings you have when you contemplate your future career? If you still feel as passionate about your ambitions, have developed new or different ones, feel more strongly than ever about the direction you want to go – ask yourself what is stopping you from reaching some of the targets you want to reach in your career. You have already demonstrated what you are capable of. There may be something that is holding you back. It might be confidence, or it might simply be that you are making assumptions about why it would not happen, rather than it can happen. Part of the purpose of reflecting back is to remind yourself about how far you have come since you first began working.

If what is holding you back is connected to being married and having a young family, it still does not mean that you cannot work as well. Women do leave work at this time in their lives, and that is their choice. This is often the time that women decide to give up their jobs because life gets complicated with small and school-age children, elderly care or both. It is known as the leaking pipeline. That should not put you off your future career aspirations though. Women's careers are not necessarily linear, and it may be that you have to compromise for a while, but many women do carry on working. They just find a different way of going and adapt.

There is a risk too that women will not be taken seriously. Assumptions are made that once a woman gets married, she will stop working anyway and have children, so what is the point of promoting her. Hamda Alshamali called on organisations to be more flexible. They needed to introduce flexi-hours and part-time working. According to Sama, companies could attract even more women into employment by extending maternity leave and allowing women to work from home more than they do now. *"This kind of flexibility will encourage women to put themselves out there."*

Keeping on track with those career ambitions to be a female senior leader takes determination, persistence and a commitment to making it work.

شُجَاعَة

CHAPTER 7

WHAT KIND OF LEADER DO YOU WANT TO BE?

In a thriving organisation, what brings people to work is not necessarily the money. It is also a sense of place and belonging, team spirit, a feeling of psychological safety similar to the criteria that Google's Project Aristotle found, and crucially a sense of purpose and meaning. Companies that flourish are those where relationships come first. Company values matter. If people do not have a sense of purpose in their work, if it has no meaning, you will not get the best out of them. Individual personal purpose might include some of the company's purpose, but everyone's personal purpose will have differences.

Leaders of organisations drive the company culture. They set the tone and standards by their behaviour and how they lead. Their personal values contribute to the culture of the organisation. When Uber's CEO and co-founder stood down in 2017 after a series of revelations about the toxic culture of the company, it transpired that he and his leadership team had devised their own list of company values and imposed them on the staff. The new CEO decided to create a fresh set of values to replace the old ones. Critically, the values were put together through collaboration with all staff so that they could contribute. For an individual employee, this alignment matters. It is the difference between going to work and enjoying every day or dreading it. Company culture is the driver of organisational strategy. The old saying 'culture eats strategy for breakfast' still holds true. You can have the best strategy, but if the culture is not right, it will not matter how good the strategic plans are, the company will not thrive.

Leadership non-negotiables

There is no 'one-size-fits-all' template for good leadership. Every leader I have come across, at any level in organisations big or small, those who I have had the privilege to work with and those who were my leaders when I first started working, all had their strengths. Some were more successful than others, and some had to work hard at it.

In my observations while coaching, facilitating, teaching and training, there are some leadership characteristics which emerge on a regular basis. These seem to either help people to lead well or will hold them back if they do not have them. These skills do not just apply to senior leaders. I think they need to be present at all levels of leadership throughout an organisation, regardless of the level of seniority. These are what I refer to as the 'leadership non-negotiables', the attributes that I think leaders need to have as part of their leadership DNA. If they do not already have them, I certainly believe they can be learned. These attributes relate to listening, self-awareness, building trust, communication and being vigilant about how they use the power of their position.

Listening

Think about how you feel when you know you are being listened to. It probably makes you feel respected and understood; that your point of view is recognised and appreciated. It helps you think. To me, the absolute priority and the most valuable asset a leader can and should have is to be able to listen and listen well. By listening well, I mean listening fully to the person who is talking and giving them your complete attention, without interruption.

I have been present in enough meetings in the Middle East to know that listening without interruption can be quite a challenge in Arab culture! Talking over each other in meetings or social gatherings is quite normal. It took me a while to adjust to this when I first started working in the region. Even so, there are times when focused and attentive listening is really essential, not just in a private meeting but also during team discussions. It is not just about listening to understand; it is also about learning from others. If you are listening well, you will notice the non-verbal cues that we all show without realising it when we talk to each other. Think about the body language of the person you are listening to. Do they look tired, energised, troubled? What is their posture like? Are they standing up straight or with shoulders hunched over? Is there something else going on that they are struggling to tell you? Just as important is the ability to listen for what is **not** being said.

Think about the last team meeting you attended. Did you get the chance to state your point of view? Did everyone say something or were there only one or two dominant voices? Was the outcome of the meeting satisfactory? How much value did you gain in attending the meeting? Did you feel listened to?

Improving the listening at team meetings can make such a difference to the efficiency of the meeting itself if everyone knows they will get the same amount of time to speak, and that decisions will not be made until everyone has been heard. It generates space and time to explore creative solutions to achieve objectives and allows the flow of different points of view, shared in a collaborative space, to tackle problems and come up with ideas for everyone's benefit. The point is that none of this will have as much impact coming from a single person as it will have coming from the diverse and collective intelligence of the team. There is a reason why we have the expression 'two heads are better than one'. Yet so often, meetings are dominated by one or two people and most of the other people who came wish they had not bothered.

Self-awareness

If you do not understand yourself and know and accept the way you are, how can you possibly understand others? Knowing yourself well means you are better able to put yourself in other's shoes, see the world from their eyes. It is not just emotional intelligence (EQ), which is about understanding yourself and your own feelings and their impact on others. It is also social intelligence (SQ). This relates to how you interact at a social level with others, how you manage complex situations and influence others to bring them with you. It means connecting brain, body and heart and developing a positive outlook which spreads throughout your team and the organisation. Successful leaders are good at this.

Finally, there is also cultural intelligence (CQ). This is the ability to work across all cultures, even if they are different from yours. All three of these kinds of intelligence are intertwined. Learning how to use them in the right way is when you will become truly effective. In terms of task-focused skills, such as following through, being detailed-orientated or preferring the big picture view, you cannot be good at everything – no one can. If you are aware that you are not strong in one area, make sure that someone in your direct leadership team is better at it than you are.

There are many ways you can raise your level of self-awareness. A Middle East client approached me to help her settle into her new role as a manager. She had worked for her company for quite a few years, and this was her first leadership position. She had previously led teams, was well organised and had a reputation for meeting her targets in good time. The company was a service provider in the region. Although she had been in the new job for a few months, she was finding it hard to get to know the team. They were not co-operating with her very well, and she was beginning to lose her nerve. Her manager was supportive and suggested she had some coaching.

After my client had summarised the situation and explained more about the relationships within the team, I suggested she might benefit from both a 360 survey and a personality assessment. A 360 is a useful way to find out what other people's perceptions are of how you are coming across. The survey is completed by colleagues, a line manager and the individual themselves. It is completed through scored answers and verbatim comments. The report is like a reflective mirror which will show what you are doing well and where there might be gaps and blind spots. You can compare your score with the scores that others have given you as well as their written comments. The key part of a good 360 report is that it is anonymous, which means that the people who complete it feel they can be honest. It provides an 'outside-in' view of how you are doing.

Completing a personality assessment helps you to understand more about your psychological self and your personal preferences – the 'inside-out' view. In our coaching sessions, we discussed the themes and patterns which emerged from the 360 to help my client understand the perspectives of her team and how she was coming across. We made links to the personality assessment, which gave her some significant insights about how she liked to work and how she reacted under pressure. My client had not appreciated that her drive to meet objectives had been overwhelming for some of her newer colleagues. She also learned that she could think fast on the spot and make decisions quickly if needed. In a crisis situation this was an asset, but sometimes she was not giving some of the team members enough time to understand her logic for the decisions she was making. They appreciated her dedication to the job, the company and her professionalism but felt she could do more to build relationships with them and communicate more regularly with them. As a result of these two assessments, she put together a list of commitments to work on over the coming months which benefited not just her but also made a big difference to the way the team worked together.

Building trust

Many leaders feel their employees should trust them first before they will trust their employees. It is the other way round. Employees need to feel trusted before they will trust. As a leader, particularly in a crisis, talking about personal concerns and worries is just as important as listening and understanding employee concerns and worries. It is fine for a leader to say that they do not know all the answers. By being more open, leaders make it normal and acceptable to show vulnerability. This openness helps to create a sense of trust. It shows leaders can empathise when colleagues come across a difficult situation. A member of the team is far less likely to feel they can be open about a crisis they might be facing if they think their manager has a problem-free life.

Leaders cannot possibly know all the answers, although many think they do. Many are reluctant to admit that they do not know what to do. The reality is that saying they do not have the solution can be liberating and it is not weak. What they do need to learn is how to ask good and insightful questions. This is the way to spark great thinking, a pooling of ideas, new ways of doing things, experimentation. It comes back to the community all the time. Leadership can be a lonely place too, especially if there are significant changes on the horizon which cannot yet be shared. It requires courage and the ability to influence. There is a fine balance between being 'leaderly' but also being open and responsive and trusting.

Communication

A further leadership skill that a leader needs to have is the ability to be able to communicate well with colleagues. This includes having open dialogue, arranging catch-up meetings, and making sure that everyone in the team or the organisation has the opportunity to ask questions about future plans and strategies. Obviously, there may be times when certain matters cannot be shared with the whole team, but creating an environment that feels open and collaborative, where everyone can communicate, reinforces the sense that everyone is working in a respectful community of adults.

Good leadership means adapting well to different situations, reading the style of leadership that is required in a given moment. It is a question of continuing to have your antennae turned on to get the sense of a situation, the feel at your fingertips and just beyond them. The Germans have a great word for this which is *'fingerspitzengefühl'*.

This kind of leadership calls for you to sense the most appropriate style depending on the situation in front of you. Can you let your team get on with it, should the decision about next steps be collaborative, do you need to tell the team what to do or can you spend time explaining what needs to be done, so they are involved in the decision?

The way you communicate will make a difference in how much the team will buy into what needs to happen, particularly when change is involved. For people to commit and accept change more positively, it is vital that they understand the 'why' behind a need for change. Too often change is implemented without enough thought being addressed to the reason for a change, why it is necessary, relevant and what is the purpose? Once this is understood, there is a much higher chance that change will be accepted. From an organisational perspective, this is a much better way to bring about change. Not only that, but the team can make suggestions about how and what can be done, collaboratively, to bring about the change.

Leadership is not the authority of your title; it is your personality that makes the difference. It is not the role that brings people with you; it is your way of being as a person that really makes the difference. In a crisis, many leaders can become controlling, hold tight to processes and not engage or communicate and certainly not discuss the uncertainty or fear about the future. At the beginning of such a crisis, it can be comforting for staff. It gives the sense that someone is in charge, and they can focus on the task because everything is too complicated. You want to know that your leader is on top of everything at a time of such upheaval. However, whilst this is fine for the short term, it is not sustainable. Instead of reducing the fear, it stokes the fires of uncertainty, creates fearfulness and builds resentment. This is the very time that communication is essential, even if, as a leader, you do not have all the answers.

The clients I have worked with who have been in more of a manager role tend to focus on the day to day tasks, ensuring that objectives are met. It is up to them to make sure that everyone in the team has clarity around their roles and responsibilities. They should also be monitoring team wellbeing, people development, and be at the centre of any fire-fighting that has to be done. Additionally, an important part of the job remit is to communicate regular constructive feedback and to talk about and celebrate team successes, not just within the team but to the manager's peers and to the boss.

Managing up as well as managing down is part of the job. What often happens is that it works well one way but not the other. A word of appreciation to the team from the head of department or the CEO goes a long way, but this will not happen if they are not informed by the manager.

Use your power wisely

In the societies of the Middle East, how power is exercised and perceived is particularly relevant in many organisations. There are wide interpretations of the meaning of power. It can range across the spectrum from coercive and forceful to persuasive and influential. Power can be overtly exercised or covertly in a secretive way, sometimes for the good and sometimes not. It also depends on whether someone takes power or has power invested in them by others. Additionally, there is systemic power in the whole organisation through custom and practice and ways of working.

The Dutch psychologist Geert Hofstede was fascinated by cross-cultural differences and developed a tool to measure power distance ratios in companies across the world. Other theorists have added to the debate over time, but the guiding principles are that the ability to speak truth to power varies in different countries around the world depending on how small or wide the distance is between those with power and those who do not have it.

Countries where there is a low power distance are those whose culture allows challenge to authority, and individuals expect to be involved in decision making. Where power distance is high, individuals do not challenge, tend to be more acquiescent and defer to authority. The culture in the Middle East can make it hard for people to challenge or ask for help from someone who is more senior than them at work. There are different kinds of power too, and in leadership it is a fine balance between wielding too much and wielding too little. Overbearing leaders do not get the best out of their people, and neither do weak ones.

Titles are important in the Middle East. Significance is attached to individual titles, and consequently, the power that the title brings them. In countries beyond the Middle East, status and recognition might more often be recognised through educational background, achievements and successes, regardless of seniority. This is not to say that these perceptions of status are absolutes.

A further aspect to take into account is that the leadership attributes most highly rated in one culture may not be the same in another. A ten-year study of the cultural attributes of 62 countries, including characteristics relating to leadership effectiveness, was published in 2004. The GLOBE study revealed that characteristics attributed to good leadership were not always consistent in every country. This was especially relevant for the Middle East. For instance, the dimension of charismatic/value-based was found by nearly all regional clusters as being a highly significant indicator of leadership excellence, except for the Middle East, where it was ranked least significant. The same pattern emerged with regard to team orientation.

One of the many criticisms of leadership theories has been that definitions of leadership excellence tend to be gender-specific, rather than gender-neutral. Historic models of leadership have been based on the qualities of male leaders and much teaching about leadership perpetuates this. This is even more pronounced in the Middle East given the nature of Arab culture. A 2012 Dubai School of Government Policy Brief drew attention to the fact that unconscious bias, explored earlier in this book, means that many people automatically think of men when thinking of leaders. Women's roles are often stereotyped as supportive, in other words, a position which will help a man to progress but without much future for the woman herself.[35] Leadership development has tended to have a Western flavour to it as if it can be slotted in regardless of culture. What is needed more than ever in MENA is a leadership development approach designed by and for this culture with some of the best global leadership practices as part of that approach.

I see more relevance of status and levels of power in my work in this region than elsewhere. Senior level leaders expect the title to command respect and unquestioned authority. I have also noticed that there are expectations about how leaders will perform in their role and how team members actually collude with this. Middle East culture and societal norms enable leaders to be autonomous without challenge. Team members are often risk-averse and fall into doing what they are told because it is an easy option and comes naturally.

This played out quite badly when I was coaching the leadership team in a client company in the GCC. A junior manager had gone on holiday, leaving one of his direct reports in charge. The temporary manager acclimatised quickly to his new authority and autonomy and made some impractical decisions. Now that he was the acting manager, he did not think he needed to seek permission to carry out his actions and his team felt unable to challenge him, even though it was a temporary situation. When the manager returned from his holiday, he overturned all the decisions, and it took some time for relationships to be repaired.

It may take a while for you to decide what leadership means for you and how you want to be as a leader. Your view may change over time. Even so, when you look at the kinds of senior roles you would like to be in and the leadership involved in them, it will be important for you to understand what leadership means to you, what your style of leadership is now or will become, and this will help you to decide if a prospective new job is right for you. If it looks like it might be suitable, consider how much capacity there would be to stretch you and your learning. If you find that you have stopped learning new things in your work, then it probably is no longer the right fit for you, and you have outgrown it. Your career should be a continuous learning experience, so be sure that any job you apply for or are offered will provide these learning opportunities and the right amount of stretch.

شُجَاعَة

CHAPTER 8

RELATIONSHIPS ARE AT THE HEART OF WHO WE ARE

Social Determination Theory was developed out of a research study by Edward Deci and Richard Ryan in 2000.[36] Put simply, the theory is closely linked to intrinsic motivation which is the drive for personal growth and achievements which are fulfilling. This kind of motivation is always about behaviour. In order to feel a sense of intrinsic motivation people need to have three specific needs fulfilled: autonomy, competence and relatedness. Autonomy means being trusted to do your job and having control over it. Competence means that you feel you are doing well at your job and being acknowledged for it. Finally, relatedness is how you relate to people around you, your interactions with them and the opportunities you have to demonstrate you hold them in positive regard and the feeling is reciprocated.

Extrinsic motivation is more about doing things for the sake of it but can also yield rewards – "If I work hard, I will get a pay rise". Either way, when leaders understand that intrinsic motivation is vital for their employees' development and enjoyment at work, they will also quickly realise what the benefits will be to the business itself. If you think about it, happier people are much nicer to be around than unhappy ones.

We are social beings. As such, our relationships are fundamental to our way of being. I think our relationships are the most important part of all our interactions in our lives. The way we develop, the way we form bonds and how we build relationships is a continuous area of study. Psychologists have identified how our brains learn patterns of behaviour through different stages as we go from childhood to adulthood. Other theories have looked at how children develop attachments to their carers, be they parents or others. These early relationships are very powerful and set the tone for how we are as adults. Sometimes they can be fractured at a young age, and the legacy of these broken relationships can live on throughout a person's life. These experiences contribute towards the formation of personality, behaviours and how we are in the world.

What happens at work

Whether someone's relationships have been difficult, joyous or a combination of both, the impact they have on personal behaviour and how well they interact with others will sometimes show up in the workplace. It is important not to always attribute someone's behaviour to the way they may have been brought up as child; it is not a simplistic process. Nevertheless, some childhood patterns are so hard-wired that they do manifest themselves in adulthood, and especially at work.

For instance, take the example of someone who has worked hard and successfully for many years and then one job is a fail. All those successes have not prepared that person for failure, and it can be a shock and take a long time to overcome. It might be someone who has worked hard at school, sometimes because they were pushed to do so by their parents. It could be that they worked hard at school because they felt they owed it to their parents to do well because they had made many sacrifices for their education. They always felt they should be top of the class and always succeeded. Sometimes, the pure ambition to succeed at school came about through lack of recognition at home or very little praise for effort. These are the people who, as adults, find it hard to measure when good is 'good enough'.

Understanding the impact of failing

Unfortunately, many people with such a strong drive to achieve and who have always been successful are completely unprepared for things to go wrong, and the repercussions of failure can be quite profound. This can cause a deep sense of shame at getting it so wrong, or anger with themselves which sometimes means they get angry with other people, or they may be embarrassed to look people in the eye. In patriarchal societies such as in the Middle East, the shame of failing is hard for men to deal with but also women.

The emotional reaction to an event like this, particularly if it has never happened in such a way before, can be overwhelming. The brain's limbic system, the emotional reaction centre, goes into overdrive. Neuroscience research has shown that the parts of the brain that are triggered by physical pain are the same as those areas of the brain that are affected by social pain. Think about the window of tolerance. Some people become aggressive under this kind of pressure, whilst others shut down or withdraw. The limbic system is responding in a 'fight, flight, freeze' way.

One of the best ways to support someone to come out of this state is by listening to them, reassuring them, acknowledging how they are feeling. This helps to activate the reward state of the brain, triggering the release of those 'feel-good' hormones like oxytocin and dopamine. If you think about a time recently when you were enjoying yourself with family and friends and feeling good, it is likely that the reward circuitry in your brain was being stimulated by these hormones. Being listened to, recognised, trusted and respected generates the same response. Of course, none of this is happening in a way that we are consciously aware of. But we know how we are feeling, and our emotional response is indicative of what is happening at an unconscious level in the brain.

When someone is feeling anxious, even if they are not admitting it, their body might be tense, and they may appear distracted and unfocused. The increasing developments in the science of the brain have shown how our brains 'talk' to each other. Being around someone who is extremely stressed can make you feel stressed as well. Without even being aware of it, in certain situations, the neurons in our brains will start to mirror what is happening in the neurons of the other person's brain. If you notice that a colleague appears to be anxious or distracted, as well as listening to them, if you relax gently back into your seat, their body will respond to this and sit back as well. Simply by physically changing their posture, they will begin to feel more at ease and start to relax.

How important are your relationships?

The relationships people have with each other provide a sense of belonging. It is a natural human need. People sometimes get put into boxes of extraversion and introversion. It is assumed that if you like being with people and enjoy a crowd that you are an extravert. And if you like being alone, dislike crowds and do not enjoy parties, you must be an introvert. In fact, it is not that simple. Extraversion and introversion relate to how you re-energise, how you recharge your batteries. Extraverts tend to like talking over their day with others, verbalising what has been happening at work, expressing their thoughts and opinions out loud. Even after a busy day at work, they are more than happy to socialise with work colleagues and friends. This is how they fill up on their energy levels. Introverts tend to respond to a busy day quite differently. They like nothing better than going home, reflecting quietly on their own and mentally processing their day. This is their way of recharging their energy levels.

What people often fail to appreciate is that just because someone is more introverted by nature, it does not mean that they do not enjoy other people's company or never go to a social event. By the same token, extraverts do not always have to be 'on'. They also enjoy their own company from time to time. Humans are a mix of personalities, preferences, types and styles. They are also carved out of all their life experiences. What they all have in common though is that they all need social interactions and relationships, even if that need is stronger in some than in others.

Family bonds are strong in all cultures and the Middle East is no exception. The pull of family is always there. Historically, much of the Middle East population existed as different tribes composed of family members, relatives and chosen favoured connections. The sense of tribe, of belonging, still matters. Outside your family, when you think about the people closest to you, it is likely that many of them will be similar to you in several ways. You will have a lot in common with the majority of your friends. There will be shared interests, a common outlook on life and the world, and there may even be people who hold a very different worldview from you, but you have a bond of friendship which embraces different points of view. These friends are like another tribe that you belong to. At work, it is the same principle. In those companies where there is a strong sense of community, collaboration and purpose, there is a sense of belonging, of family. You are part of this tribe as well.

Relationships at work

At any level, and especially if you want to move into a leadership role, a first step must be to reflect on whether the organisation you are in is a good fit for you. Companies change. What first drew you to the organisation may no longer exist. The company may have grown too big. It could have been taken over, and the culture may no longer suit you. You might have changed too. In the same way that you feel a sense of belonging with your family and your friends, feeling that you belong where you work and that it is a good fit for you will bring out the best in you at work.

Relationships at work are just as important as they are outside work. People who enjoy their job have a sense of meaning about what they do. They do not come to work just for their salary. They are loyal to their place of work, often feel pride in being an employee of a particular organisation and have a great sense of relationship with their colleagues. On average, people spend nearly a third of their lives working. You should expect that it is a good place to be and do your level best to make sure it is. It is all part of our connections. The animal kingdom is no different. Herds stay together, socialise together and have their own tribes too.

When you think about organisations that are successful, of course, the business ability of the leadership is key to that success. However, it is not just that. It is also linked to how the leadership have connected with the workforce, how the people in those companies have responded and what kind and quality of relationships have been formed within the organisation. Equally, if you look at companies which have failed, it is not just about lack of profits. There will often be a story there about how the leadership either lost its connection or never fully made one with its employees.

In contrast, during the pandemic, many stories emerged about companies struggling to survive where the staff continued to work on less pay to try and keep things going. Of course, those employees did not want to lose their jobs. But they were also prepared to keep trying to find a way through because of the bonds of relationships that existed in those companies. They did not want to lose those connections either.

Having presence in your relationships

What I notice in the leaders I work with is that those who thrive and create a flourishing and committed workforce also have something called presence. It is not simply that they are present in the room or space. Just being in a meeting is easy enough and means you are present. Presence is more than that. It is about bringing your whole self to each interaction, each meeting, each encounter. Presence is a way of being. From the moment you arrive, you are there, focused, listening and giving attention to everyone around you. It can be loud presence or quiet presence. This sense of presence is not just confined to leaders though. Many people have this, regardless of their role or what they do, whether they work or not.

Not everyone wants to become a leader, be it leading a team of one or two people or running a company. But if you do, you need to have presence or find a way of developing it. Again and again, it comes back to relationships. Presence helps to forge good relationships, and these relationships are the foundation of successful organisations.

Imagine yourself coming into a room for a meeting. Reflect on how you enter the room. Do you arrive early, on time, or are you often late? Be honest about it! When you come into the room, do you close the door as quickly as possible, grab the nearest empty seat and drop your notebook, mobile phone, perhaps a drink, on the table? Or do you scan the room quickly before you sit down? When you join this meeting, do you think about how loudly or quietly you need to close the door, or do you just close it? Do you notice if anyone is speaking? All these questions relate to what is called the emotional wake that you are creating as you enter the room, and while you are there.

Reflect on the way you show up, how you make people feel, do you communicate well, are you curious about other points of view, are you asking good questions and explaining why things need to be done, not just the what and the how? After the meeting, assess the impression you made with colleagues and clients and the impact you have created. All of these things contribute to your emotional wake. This wake is another element of presence.

The extra essence that a good leader brings to an organisation relates to the quality of their presence and how it shows up. Good leadership is demonstrated through actions, not the badge or title of the role. It comes through in the way that people listen and pay attention to what someone is saying. It shows in the transparency of communications in an organisation. Actively noticing everyone's contribution, briefly stopping to chat to someone as you walk past them, treating everyone as equal – it is these small nuances and gestures which make the difference between an average leader and a good one. This is what builds trusted relationships. Even if you are not yet ready for a senior leadership role, it is never too early to practise some of these behaviours.

شُجَاعَة

CHAPTER 9

A COLLABORATION BETWEEN ALL GENDERS

Many of the debates that have taken place in the past several decades and that still happen now about women and leadership have focused on the disparity between opportunities for men and those for women to move into leadership positions. These leadership roles can be in all parts of an organisation, not just at senior levels.

Now that more countries are beginning to have diverse boards, much research has been done on whether this makes a difference to company profits and other growth areas. We know already that women bring different perspectives on decision making. It seems to me that this is looking at this from the wrong end of the telescope. Looking at the cost-benefits is a useful and important aspect to encourage more diverse boards. However, the bottom line is that half the population are women and half men. Therefore boards should have a 50/50 split too, and there should be no need to justify the benefits of having women on boards. They should be there anyway. To my knowledge, there has never been any attempt at justifying why there are male board members.

Getting all genders involved

The polarisation of opinions already discussed might suggest that there is only one way to approach this issue, which is just to keep working on delivering more and more opportunities for women to move into leadership roles in the Middle East. Whilst this is definitely the case, the truth is that none of these changes can be brought about by women on their own, and men have to be included in the change in mindset. I am concerned when I hear men being described in negative ways in some organisations or stereotyped as being difficult or awkward. This is not about men being bad and women being good.

Men and women are different, and this is why gender is such an important topic. For any fundamental and long-lasting changes to be assured, men have to be part of this whole conversation and have their voices heard too. We should be able to reach a stage where people achieve their career aspirations based solely on ability and applicability for the role. The Middle East is not there yet, and it is what happens right now that will either speed this up or slow things down.

As already discussed, unconscious bias has a large part to play in how women have progressed through their careers compared with men. Historically, and certainly at the beginning of the Industrial Revolution in Europe and America, women were working. They may have been in what would now be classified as menial roles such as labouring on farms and fledgling manufacturing industries, but they were earning money. This began to change as the growth of a new merchant class was born out of the manufacturing industry as it expanded. Some of these merchants, mostly men, became wealthy in a comparatively short period of time. Showing this wealth in society became important, and one way to do this was by having a wife who did not have to work. Wives who had leisure time to meet with friends and socialise provided visual evidence of a man's wealth. In certain cultures and societies, this is still the case.

The picture in the UAE is quite advanced in respect of women's roles. In just a short time in the UAE's history, the government has sought to propel the Emirates into the modern world. The expression 'women hold up half the sky' has been heard frequently over many years, and the opportunities for women have been considerable. They also have some freedoms which are not found in some of the UAE's neighbours.

Why the delay?

What is holding back the progression for many women, in spite of government initiatives, is the bottleneck at senior levels in organisations. This applies across the region.

Many CEOs have been in their position for a very long time. The pace of change has been so fast that it has been difficult for some men from more traditional backgrounds to adjust, particularly if either their wives or some of the women in their families do not work. Change itself takes adjusting to at different paces for different people. Where there is a lot of change in a comparatively short time span, adapting to it quickly can be difficult. When it goes to the core of how people have been brought up and the cultural background that they have, accepting change can be slow, and some people may never adjust.

For men in the region, the rise of women can be seen as a threat to their status. In the Arab world, as we know, this sense of status is very important. I have spoken about this to many male nationals in the region. Anecdotally, they say they often feel sidelined, left on the fringes, and perceive themselves to be in an 'out-group' while women are currently in the 'in-group'. They can also get frustrated by the attention being paid to women's development, and feel it takes away from any focus on their own job progression. For many men, the adjustment to accepting full equality between men and women is not about seeing women as inferior. It relates more to their upbringing and expectations. After all, many have been living in a man's world for a very long time. They need to change, but there is often resistance to change. It is also about loss of control and fear of the unknown. Women do not always help themselves either. Their behaviour can be hostile towards male colleagues and dismissive. Some have also grown a sense of entitlement, an idea that promotion into a leadership role is their right.

The reality is that supporting women to move into more senior and leadership roles cannot be achieved without the support of men. It is a collaboration between all genders, and women cannot do this in isolation. Sheryl Sandberg, Chief Operating Officer of Facebook, describes this as 'coalitions of support'.[37]

Training initiatives

As well as providing courses for women, it could be helpful to offer company-wide training and understanding of unconscious bias for both women and men, even in those companies where there are no apparent gender biases. We all have biases and reminding people about them helps to normalise them. It also embeds a company practice to work hard on drawing attention to them, raising awareness in managing them, and using different language to increase diversity and inclusion.

Linda Al Ali thought this was particularly relevant in Jordan, *"Organisations must develop a culture that values women and calls out bias and men should be involved in leading and nurturing this charge."* She said this could be achieved provided diversity and inclusion training took place frequently and systematically. The training should focus on *"…strategies to change long-term behaviours."* The important thing for Shaikha Ahmad, an Emirati Senior Planning and Design Engineer, was that leaders and decision makers needed to sponsor these initiatives. What helped was that *"…the international movements and listings have incentivised government to bring about change, not fall behind."* In companies that do not have equal opportunities for promotions, Shaikha felt inclusion and diversity training needed to be built on regularly and some kind of measurement about the gender balance of recruitment would be good. The leadership would also need to give their support to unbiased progression.

There is little impact if any training just becomes a tick-box exercise. Unfortunately, in some companies this is what happens. The need to do it has been acknowledged, it has been carried out and it ends there. Following unconscious bias training, once there is understanding and awareness, discussion groups, which include men and women with a facilitator, can help to share experiences and perspectives in an open way. For some people, it may never have occurred to them that there might be a different perspective from their own, not through any disregard but just not thinking about it. In any organisation, these events have to be championed at a senior level. Rather than making women and leadership a separate issue, it should be integrated into the way businesses work.

Aisha (not her real name) is Emirati and Head of Marketing in her organisation. Her company has clear development paths for women, but she acknowledged this was probably because it is an MNC. She also thought that men could be doing more to support women's development but appreciated that *"cultural norms and stereotypes are also difficult to bridge — so, international exposure to further encourage change would be helpful."*

There are government schemes in some countries which offer funding for continuing education abroad. Organisations need to support these schemes, and this can have its benefits too. Maha Bin Hendi studied for her Law degree in London and her Master's in Law in New York but felt that she had benefited through her international experience by learning new skills. *"It was not easy working abroad, dealing with people from different backgrounds and the level of seniority was all a learning curve for me, especially when I was new to the working field at the time."* Farah found her international experience invaluable. She had an internship in Singapore with a global span of architectural projects. *"My training was challenging yet interesting in terms of multi-tasking and exposure to different departments."*

Harnessing talent

HH Dr Basma thought that women should not be afraid to ask for help. She advised women not to complain but rather to use storytelling as a powerful way to express their feelings saying it had much more of a lasting impact. *"It's much stronger than using anger and a loud voice."* She recommended using the energy of anger as a force for good. To any suggestion that it was harder for women to have a voice if they were not in a similar position as hers, HH Dr Basma said it depended completely on other people's perceptions and her view was that she was able to use her position to influence precisely because she did have a voice.

Using storytelling, women can switch the argument to talking about leveraging diversity and differences as a business benefit, not just for women and men individually, but also the team and the organisation. Ultimately, it is about developing talent everywhere.

Fatima (not her real name), a Saudi Arabian national, stated that in her organisation there was only one female leader, and women needed to fight more for what they wanted. Communications could be improved between men and women to support their development. Although things in the Kingdom have opened up, including the appointment of Ambassadors, she wanted to see that women were being given more chances and be trusted to lead. This was echoed by Linda Al Ali, who wanted to see more development opportunities being offered by organisations. *"Offering constructive pathways and training to help high-potential employees grow can create a strong pipeline for female leadership."*

There are many descriptions of the function of developing talent and managing people in organisations. People are the greatest asset of any business, and I find the functional titles such as Human Resources (I often hear this referred to as 'Human Remains') or Human Capital quite clinical. It makes people sound like units and quite the opposite of human beings. The same function might be called Talent, Personnel, People Resources, or even just People. Whatever the description is, someone senior from this function should be a co-pilot in the whole project. Male senior directors and board level members need to be involved too, and this is the only way these initiatives will be taken seriously.

It is imperative that change in organisations is cascaded from the top, and the best persuaders to bring men into this way of thinking are probably other men who are already championing the change. Women in mid-level can gather to create experiments, come up with suggestions through the process of Adaptive Leadership and take responsibility for what they need to do to push forward. This is not about waiting for changes to happen but stepping into the situation and forming small groups to make a difference, and then showing evidence about how things might develop for women in the organisation. To manage the risk that men may feel sidelined, include them in working committees or focus groups.

The business benefit

Joining together to show how women's contributions can have a transformative impact on teams and the organisation is the way forward. The reason all this matters is that there is a business benefit. It is not about winning or losing position or status. The focus is on collaboration and how strengths can be fully utilised, not just those of women employees but also those of male employees. In the MENA region, there are varying opportunities to do this depending on the country. Regional averages indicate that whilst women are doing well with access to health and education, they are doing much less well in many countries on economic and political empowerment.

In 2013, the World Bank described this is as the 'MENA Paradox' or the 'MENA Puzzle'.[38] In other words, where you would expect all of these elements to be in balance in each country, they are not. Five years later, the Institute of Labour Economics (2018) issued a further study which indicated that the 'MENA Paradox' still persists.[39] In 2019, only a fifth of MENA women were employed or job-hunting, and they were adding less than a fifth to the region's GDP. Just imagine the difference that it would make to the overall GDP if women's employment figures were doubled or trebled.

As well as the MENA Paradox, it is worth considering what is known as the 'Paula Principle', an idea developed by Tom Schuller in 2017.[40] Based on the older 'Peter Principle' which suggested that every male employee reached his own level of ineffectiveness, the 'Paula Principle' explains that most women are working below their level of effectiveness. Schuller suggests the causes include lack of confidence and gender discrimination.

Randa explained that the criteria for successful job candidates in Jordan were based on experience, seniority and support from people in positions of authority. Consequently, *"Organisations should invest more in their personnel by providing more training opportunities to empower qualified women to get to leadership roles and strive to make a gender balance."* There should be more development programmes targeted at women. They would also be helped by a supportive line manager, regardless of gender, as well as their husbands.

Several of the women I spoke to had attended official leadership development programmes which had a positive impact. These included Adaptive Leadership, their own company's internal programme, and a UAE government programme. Separately, courses had included a Project Management Training Course (PMT), Emotional Intelligence, Team Management, Neuro-Linguistic Programming (NLP), and Business Ethics. Several had found their higher education and business school experiences powerful, and learning on the job had been more beneficial than anything. Out of all the women who have contributed to this book, only one had not had any training offered to her. To an extent, I found this encouraging. When I explored this same topic in 2017, there were far fewer opportunities being offered.

Nevertheless, given the number of comments now about the need to increase leadership development programmes for women, it seems that many company policies still lack the will or do not feel the need to implement these policies for development. There is also a mixed picture about how much some organisations are willing to start discussions about it.

Hiba pointed out that in her organisation, negotiating stakeholder relationships was the key to progression for both women and men. *"He/she needs to manage stakeholders up, down, and sideways, perform well, and exhibit success. Women, I find, are less potent in exhibiting success, while men brag about the smallest achievements."*

Government intervention

There is a lack of coherent information across the region about women's empowerment platforms that have been established by individual governments. There are umbrella organisations which offer programmes for women and institutions, such as the EU and the UN who are supporting several projects for women in the region. Jordan, Lebanon and Morocco have established alliances to help women's empowerment but perhaps not with the same fanfare or publicity as in the UAE.

The UAE government initiatives which have been launched since the Dubai Women Establishment in 2006 and later have made some difference. The clarity around this government support and how much various government ministers have spoken about it publicly somehow seems to have given women permission to fight harder for recognition at work and opportunities to develop their leadership skills. My 2017 research found that although some companies were in part supporting women to develop their leadership skills by offering training programmes, there was frustration as well about how much they still felt they were being held back, not so much by their families but by their organisations. Between 2017 and 2020, there were some changes, but even so, there seemed still more to do.

Many of the women I have spoken to in the region during the last three years are frustrated about the barriers that continue to exist. They may have improved for them personally, but they are acutely aware that access to any kind of training and development varies considerably, not just across MENA but also within countries.

There was a variety of ideas from the women I interviewed for this book about what should be happening in government, society, and what more women could do for themselves. In respect of the UAE, Lina Farajallah said that 62% of women are unemployed. Even though they had a lot to offer in the workplace, too many were having to leave before they were ready because norms and traditions were putting pressure on them to do so. As well as increasing childcare, Lina felt that both the government and the private sector should be encouraging equal wages in order to *"...fit in with the modernisation of industrial relations to help increase women in the workforce and in leadership roles."* She also thought that faith leaders should be doing more to reverse past amendments to religious laws which removed the rights of women to be equal to those of men and that *"...religion should be self-centred rather than publicly forced."*

Organisations should be recruiting managers who make the most of women's potential rather than discourage it, stated Hiba, *"From my observation, women tend to be a lot more self-critical, and sometimes they need to be pushed to grow."*

Although Natalia appreciated that change would be slow, she thought that women taking more of the responsibility to drive their ambitions forward would also encourage mass media attention. There would be a knock-on effect in education so that the next generation accepted that gender inequality would be a thing of the past.

Alia Al Nabooda considered that women had to take more control over their development. *"I think women should build themselves up to be capable to handle a leadership role by enrolling in leadership courses and building their technical expertise in their field. They should be determined and confident and push through to get what they want."*

The challenge for men

The centuries-old tradition of patriarchy in the Middle East and powerful societal values which were defined by Islamic beliefs continues to have a tight grip on some societies, even today. Boys and girls, men and women – all had their roles. Expectations for young boys were that they would be leaders in adulthood, that they would be in charge and would have authority over women. There is a great sense of honour, self-respect and pride, loyalty to friends and family. At work, some of these men may have been in their jobs for quite a long time, and the more conservative among them struggle with the idea that women are even working. They adhere to the strict regulations of their faith that women should be at home looking after the house and family.

There comes an even bigger challenge for some of these men when young women not only come into the workplace but also get promoted over them. It is not simply a question of having to take orders from a more junior, and possibly in their eyes, less experienced person. This dynamic goes against all the traditional expectations that these men may have had about working women. Not only that, some women find it hard to manage a male direct report who might be older than they are. Culturally, age and maturity are respected and valued. This is a paradox that many women in the region are facing on a regular basis. On the one hand, they feel entitled to be a manager, and on the other hand, they are coming up against a situation which contradicts their upbringing. Both the manager and the subordinate can end up having polarised positions. The situation can take on the appearance of a difficult 'authoritarian father/difficult daughter' relationship. This can spread into a toxic environment for colleagues, and in my coaching work, this scenario has played out over and over again. Sometimes it can seem that the only recourse is official mediation.

Unless things change in organisations, there is a risk of loss of resource and the departure of a group of talented, motivated and highly educated women who either go to organisations where they know they will be valued, or they set up on their own. There are growing numbers of women now doing this, although the figures are much lower compared with many other countries around the world. Differences in lines of business vary and might depend on the motivations behind setting up their own enterprises. Some women do not necessarily have a financial imperative to support the income of the family, and their businesses may be a personal interest. However, you only have to look at the statistics for women entrepreneurs to see how well represented they are becoming in the Middle East.

Al Masah Capital[41] carried out a study into the rise of female entrepreneurship in small and medium-sized businesses, especially in GCC countries where they are well supported by their respective governments. The study indicated that the reasons contributing to their success included better access to education and a gradual change in cultural norms in some of the GCC countries but not all. There needs to be more access to education and fewer social limitations for all women. There is an increasing rise in technology and innovation startups, and these successful businesses have a lot to contribute to the economy.

Even MNCs cannot escape the impact of culture. They may have aspects of the style of the parent company, but even so, there will be clear indications that the regional culture is ever-present in the environment. Yet there are senior women running companies, there are some who are board directors, and there are others who have worked hard and broken through whatever their company's version of the 'glass ceiling' is. There are also senior women in government in several countries. It would be invidious to suggest that all these successful women have moved into these positions just because of their connections or sponsors, or government initiatives to increase diversity at senior level and board quotas in some countries.

The drive by some governments to ensure that most jobs are held by nationals, rather than expatriates, may not have helped in some ways. It has given a licence to some men to challenge recruitment decisions which makes the push for diversity even more complicated than it already is. Locally owned companies, as well as MNCs, have to demonstrate that their hiring decisions are based on nationality first and foremost. Governments are seeking to ensure that nationals are employed as a priority and want to limit the number of expatriate workers. This is also the case at CEO level. Many expatriates have accepted that however well they have achieved profits and growth, and no matter how well their organisation may be flourishing during their tenure, they are unlikely to be appointed as group CEO or Chairman or Chairwoman.

شُجَاعَة

CHAPTER 10

IT IS YOUR WAY OF BEING THAT MATTERS

Your way of being is how you have developed as a person from childhood through to adulthood with many different influences. You are already aware of how these cultural influences affect how companies are run, the hierarchy and social expectations of behaviour. This means that some of those ways of being are highly visible in the workplace, and this includes how women progress in organisations, especially those that are locally owned and locally run, as well as some government entities.

The global pandemic ushered in many changes to our familiar world, how we were living out our lives and our expectations of the future. What is ahead may remain unpredictable and uncertain for a long period of time. I am sure the reality and the echo of Covid-19 will be with us for the rest of our lives. I am also sure this echo will follow through into the next generation and the ones after that. There have been terrible personal tragedies and loss, irrevocable damage to global businesses, and repercussions which we may not yet fully appreciate, not least the impact on mental health. However, the crisis has also provided an opportunity to take a look at how we work and interact, and find new meaning and purpose in our lives, or even confirm that our dreams and aspirations still apply, even now.

Changing your approach

Going through change is tough, especially when it has been imposed by external factors and you have no control over it. Many people follow a similar pattern as they come to terms with change. There is often a great sense of loss about what is past, refusing to accept things need to change, and that their lives are no longer predictable. The main point about change is that you will not be able to move through it unless and until you actually accept it. Once you get to this point of acceptance, the energy you have used to fight change can be turned into positive energy to help you rebuild. This pattern can often feel the same with changes at work. If you are feeling discouraged by what is ahead of you, particularly if you were already finding it hard to progress your career, try standing back and looking at your options with a bit more distance.

A unique culture

When I think about the difference in the way of working in the Middle East compared with say Europe, the US or Asia, it seems clear to me that so much of working and daily life is informed by the culture. To my mind, it is quite different from any other region that I have experienced. Perhaps it is because other regions are more diverse internationally, but I do not think that is the reason. After all, there are many nationalities living and working in the Middle East. I think it is more that Arab culture is intertwined with organisational culture and this blend of tradition, culture and faith is what makes the difference. I believe organisational culture has grown out of this belief system through the centuries, and this is why this culture is unique to the Middle East. Added to this, each country in MENA has its own country-specific culture.

The crucible of the Muslim faith is Mecca in Saudi Arabia. It became established through the teachings of the Prophet Mohammed, who was born in the year 571 CE. Islamic faith and culture took hold from those times. In spite of these origins, the largest population of Muslims in the world are found in Indonesia, not the Middle East; 82% of Indonesia's population is Muslim.

Interestingly, it would appear that Indonesian culture does not manifest itself in the same way as it does in the Middle East. Although there is evidence of Muslims existing in Indonesia in the 8th century, it was not until Muslim traders began travelling east around the 13th century that it began to take hold, particularly in Indonesia. By then, various secular religions were already established, and the culture has evolved through integration with these religions. This why it is different from the Middle East.

The other difference is the democratisation of Indonesia which began in 1950. There are strong influences of Sharia in Indonesian laws and regulations, and some parts of the country are conservative in the way they practise Islam, but secular religions still have strong roots in the culture. Currently, there is a powerful push by women towards gender equality and putting an end to violence against women. The figures are not substantive as there is no official data for the country. Latest estimates suggest that approximately a third of the female population have already or are currently experiencing violence in some form.[42]

The external view of the Middle East

Some people unfamiliar with the Middle East see it as one amorphous region, although they will happily discuss the differences in countries within Europe or Latin America. They also accept that there are differences in country profiles and cultural characteristics in these regions. As far as MENA is concerned, they sometimes have fixed views, often incorrect, about the place of women and are surprised and amazed when they hear about how many successful working women there are and what they have achieved.

The pace of change may seem inconceivably slow when compared with other countries outside MENA.

This ignores the rich and often dramatic history of the region and the geopolitical changes that occurred at the beginning of the 20th century. Since then, the Middle East has been in a state of flux, with considerable tensions that are still ongoing in some countries, and underlying it all, the growing public clash between traditionalism and modernism. Young people are pushing against the rules and seeking more independence. This, in itself, may well create more opportunities for women to speak out.

The issue of connections through networking is problematic in the Middle East. There is still a lack of mixed networking in a business context. These networks which create in the moment and offline conversations, advanced warning about possible openings, and opportunities for impromptu introductions, are not as prevalent as they are outside the region. This can be frustrating for women who want to progress and move forward on their own two feet by their personal endeavours and not through familial connections alone. The growing independence women have found through their educational choices has been hard fought, and hard won and they are reluctant to lose this sense of empowerment. In order to keep this growing sense of autonomy and independence, or start creating it, what more can you do to move forward with your dreams?

Use your culture

This is where the culture of the region can be used as a mechanism for female leadership empowerment. Instead of pushing against the culture, you could adapt and use it to your advantage. Going back to the idea of the wise elders, engaging those men in their discussions and using their knowledge – not being too proud to ask for it – may be part of a step forward. After all, many of these men have been running companies for a long time, know quite a bit about business, and perhaps it is an opportunity for them to feed this forward. This may be a way to demonstrate that they continue to be needed. The age range for many men in senior roles in organisations and government entities goes up to retirement age. This can be where some of the obstructions are to progression. It creates a block while they mark out their time before they leave. Their successor has to wait, which can create a knock-on effect at all levels.

By encouraging these senior employees to share their expertise and knowledge, you might be helping them to overcome some of the concerns and worries many people, both men and women, face as they approach retirement. Some of these worries are often about feeling lost and without purpose, no longer required or useful, wondering how they will fill their time. Critically, many who are approaching retirement will experience a loss of status. This is a fascinating aspect of Arab culture. Arab men and women are very proud people. They are proud of their nationality, their culture, their religion and their identity. This kind of pride is also linked to how they are seen by others, and job title and positions in the hierarchy contribute to their sense of status. You can acknowledge their status by tapping into their wisdom and years of experience.

There are many more examples which demonstrate how much culture is intertwined with all aspects of working and personal life. Acknowledging this and using senior wisdom in organisations is one way to develop greater understanding of different perspectives. There are already formidable challenges. One thing not to be forgotten is that younger men and women coming into work will have different ideals and parameters about what working life should look like for them. There are likely to be headwinds too with the next generation. Far better to have organisational systems in place now that can be flexible and absorb the evolving patterns of work.

What else can organisations do to support you to move into leadership positions? Leadership development programmes are a good place to start. But you need to ask for them, or for training workshops. As well as offering programmes for women, programmes should be offered to men as well. If nothing is set up for them, there is a risk that they will think female employees are being singled out for special treatment, or that they need fixing. Men need development programmes too.

The content is the key to changing mindsets. One way is to include topics such as emotional and social intelligence, negotiating and influencing, and presentation skills. Team exercises with men and women would encourage discussions and the opportunity to see things from different perspectives. Gender diversity as well as diversity of opinions is something to be embraced, not fought against. This is where the richness of organisational output comes from. Ideas that are pooled, shared and explored have a much higher likelihood of success than single solutions to every problem.

If there is a preference to have women-only leadership development programmes, and there is some merit in this, particularly to shift some of the organisational cultures where women are being held back, companies can be supported in designing bespoke leadership development and training programmes specifically for women. It is essential with these kinds of programmes that they are not seen to be creating 'mini-me' versions of male colleagues. Rather, they should be seen as developing the individual. The best way to ensure this is to offer similar training to male employees. It is also another way to avoid resentment, and in any case, any staff development is a good benefit for the organisation. Ultimately, all staff with the potential to be future leaders should have these opportunities because they merit it, and there should be no distinctions. You never know how successful you might be at getting what you want just by starting the conversation.

You might suggest that your organisation could create learning hubs which would provide opportunities for all employees to share their experiences and hear each other's points of view about what it is like to make these shifts. While you might have strong evidence of bias against you, there may not be many opportunities for men not only to hear about this but also share how they feel when organisational shifts mean coming to terms with a different way of looking at gender equality.

None of these changes can happen without the input of the top leadership. Their sponsoring of these events, modelling the same behaviours and having and enabling open and honest conversations in a psychologically safe environment will go a long way to effecting a change in culture. They also control the budgets, and it is up to them to see this as a capital expenditure, even if they need persuading. I have worked in many organisations on leadership development programmes where the participants fully accept that change needs to happen but are blocked in making those changes by the top management. This can be demoralising, but it is also up to those individuals to make change happen from within. This means driving forward initiatives, however small, to create a different way of going. Experimenting with change, rather than imposing it, is the best way forward. The ripples will spread out, and the positive impact can gather momentum all of its own.

Open communication about success stories can make a big difference and helps to create an environment where it is OK to speak out and express an opinion in a constructive manner. This also reduces the damaging effects of silos in organisations when people withdraw into their own areas and do not share or encourage good collaboration between teams and departments. Work becomes a competition, blaming others for problems begins to build, and this negativity creates toxicity in the environment. Once this is established, it takes a lot of work to get rid of it.

What next for you?

There are some advocates who have been involved in global campaigns to remove the adjective 'women' from networks. Their view is that networks are about people and should not be gender-defined. In societies where this is

SHUJAA'AH

possible that might be a reasonable idea for discussion. It is difficult in some parts of the Middle East. The conditions are not yet there in many countries for women to even begin building networks, and that has to be the place to start, even if the ambition is to have access to the currently 'all male' networks. Women need to keep building these networks and not be put off even if it is difficult. There is power in the group. These networks enable knowledge sharing, understanding what other women did to get where they wanted to. In some Middle Eastern states, the government support for women is a great ticket to set up networks and drive some initiatives to support each other. You have permission to do this, and it is empowering. That permission is a useful rebuttal against resistance. There is no reason why you cannot go forward and create these group conversations for yourself.

Whilst there are many networks for women across the region, there are far fewer that focus on business for women. Morocco, Lebanon, Saudi Arabia, Dubai and Abu Dhabi have several. There are very few in Kuwait, Bahrain and Jordan. There are also umbrella networking associations for women with local representation. It is true that some women need the support of their families to be able to go out and network.

If you are unable to find any, think about creating your own small one with like-minded women that you already know, or connect with them through social media platforms such as LinkedIn. It can be easier if it is with other women as a place to start. This is about making the most of the situation with regard to what can be controlled, rather than what cannot.

152

If there are entrepreneurial events taking place locally for women, think about whether you could ask your company to sponsor one. Even if they refuse, it could still be worth you attending even if you think this is not ideal for you. It is a good place to hear about how women have started up their own businesses, what encouragement they needed, what problems they dealt with, and what helped them. Not all these women will have had family support, and some may have launched their own businesses to generate an income and to support their families. Being able to work from home will have helped some of them to manage work and family life as well. There would be learning for you about how they managed the conversations and how they raised their confidence levels to launch into a business that was their own. You could also use the opportunity to build new relationships.

Build a relationship with a sponsor

I think mentoring has its place and can be effective. However, I think what will really drive women's leadership development in organisations and what is sorely needed is senior sponsors, particularly men. Remember that changes in the way organisations support women's leadership development need to come from the top. Accept the fact that you will need support from men. It is the senior people who can nurture your leadership development, track your career progress and encourage you. Significantly, if they are men, they are best placed to persuade other men in the organisation to do the same. They become champions of talented female employees, and it is out in the open.

Dr Robert Cialdini (2007) has studied extensively on the psychology of influencing and persuading and calls this 'Social Proof'.[43] In other words, if peers see another peer being acknowledged for something that demonstrates their expertise, they are much more likely to do the same thing. This 'Social Proof' also relates to your female colleagues. It sends a message loud and clear that they can be sponsored as well if they are willing to put themselves out there.

Always keep in mind the importance of relationships. If you do not know any of the senior people in your organisation very well, find a colleague who could advise you on who would be the best person to speak to. Build the relationship. This is all about you and helping him/her to get to know you. It is about how you are coming across as a person. If you can be yourself in all of the conversations you initiate as you expand your network, your abilities and desire for learning will come through. People will remember you for how you connected. This is what I mean by 'the way of being'.

The necessary shift from relying on oil revenues to support public finances has resulted in several government measures, including increased taxes like VAT, particularly in the GCC. There was already disquiet that it would mean cutbacks for government development programmes for women. These concerns were heightened as GCC governments announced further budgetary restraints after the pandemic to protect business in the region.[44]

It will be tough and take several years to get things back on track. It will also be an opportunity to create exciting visions across the globe that embrace equality and diversity in new and different ways. The world will need leaders who are brave and courageous and eager to be part of a new world. MENA is no exception. It also has a major advantage over so many other countries and regions because, in spite of various in-country crises, there is already a tremendous growth culture in the region and exciting new visions with all the opportunities they will bring. Women are still an untapped resource in the region, and their leadership can and should be at the centre of this growth.

Final reflections

All the women who contributed to this book had insightful and inspirational suggestions about what women in MENA can do to keep on track towards their leadership goals. I would like to leave you with some more to reflect on.

"Know where you want to be in life."

"Once you show your potential in the course of your work, your chance of growth is there – individuals can create their own career path."

"Be more supportive of other women when they are on the journey and reach the top."

"Do more tasks that involve decision making… it leads to organisational growth as a whole."

"Continue obtaining the qualifications, education and experience for target roles."

"Understand that to drive inclusion, we too need to be inclusive and support change."

"Build a network with higher up people to pull you up and give you feedback."

"Subscribe to courses to help build confidence and leadership skills."

"Silence negative self-talk."

"Keep going when the going gets tough."

"You have the will and power."

By just being yourself you can also take advantage of all the creative and different openings that are ahead of you. You may not be there – yet. But you can be, and you deserve it provided you choose to commit. Be ***shujaa'ah!***

ENDNOTES

1   Harper, A. (2017), *Token Evolution or Real Revolution: The Impact of the United Arab Emirates Government Initiatives for Women and their Leadership Development* (Submitted as part of MA Degree in Middle Eastern Studies, King's College, London 2017).

2   Hertog, S. (2018, July 25). *The Political Decline and Social Rise of Tribal Identity in the GCC.* London School of Economics (LSE) https://blogs.lse.ac.uk/mec/2018/07/25/the-political-decline-and-social-rise-of-tribal-identity-in-the-gcc/

3   World Economic Forum Global Gender Gap Report 2020. https://reports.weforum.org/global-gender-gap-report-2020

4   Harper, A. (2017), *Token Evolution or Real Revolution: The Impact of the United Arab Emirates Government Initiatives for Women and their Leadership Development* (Submitted as part of MA Degree in Middle Eastern Studies, King's College, London 2017).

5   Gulf Labour Markets and Migration; Latest Data 2010-2016 https://gulfmigration.org/

6   Assaad, R., Barsoum, G. *Public employment in the Middle East and North Africa.* IZA World of Labor 2019: 463 doi: 10.15185/izawol.463

7   World Economic Forum Global Gender Gap Report 2020. https://reports.weforum.org/global-gender-gap-report-2020

8   McKinsey & Co (2018, 31 January): *"Why you need a CTO - and how to make her successful."* https://www.mckinsey.com/business-functions/operations/our-insights/why-you-need-a-cto-and-how-to-make-her-successful#

9   Bennis, N. W. (1985). *Leaders: The Strategies for Taking Charge* (First ed.). Harper Perennial.

10   Heifetz, R. A., Linsky, M., & Grashow, A. (2009). *The Practice of Adaptive Leadership: Tools and Tactics for Changing Your Organization and the World* (1st ed.). Harvard Business Press.

11   Bill Gates (2018, December 29): *"What I learned at work this year."* https://www.gatesnotes.com/About-Bill-Gates/Year-in-Review-2018

12   Walter Isaacson (2012, April): *"The Real Leadership Lessons of Steve Jobs."* Harvard Business Review. https://hbr.org/2012/04/the-real-leadership-lessons-of-steve-jobs

13   Tariq A. Al Maeena (2018, June 30). Gulf News Opinion: *"Rising Arab divorce rates a cause for concern."* https://gulfnews.com/opinion/op-eds/rising-arab-divorce-rates-a-cause-for-concern-1.2244451

14   https://rework.withgoogle.com/guides/understanding-team-effectiveness

15   Arab News (2019, May 14): *"The Hidden Face of Mental Illness in the Middle East."* https://www.arabnews.com/node/1496661/middle-east

16   UK Office of National Statistics Report: *Gender pay gap in the UK: 2019*
https://www.ons.gov.uk/employmentandlabourmarket/peopleinwork/earningsandworkinghours/bulletins/genderpaygapintheuk/2019

17   Eurostat Statistics Explained 2020
https://ec.europa.eu/eurostat/statistics e x p l a i n e d / index.php?title=Wages_and_labour_costs#Gender_pay_gap

18   Babcock, L., & Laschever, S. (2003). *Women Don't Ask: Negotiation and the Gender Divide.* Princeton University Press.

19   Hannah Riley Bowles, Bobbi Thomason, & May Al Dabbagh, (2017, September 8): *"When Men Have Lower Status at Work, They're Less Likely to Negotiate."* Harvard Business Review. https://hbr.org/2017/09/research-low-status-men-hesitate-to-negotiate-their-salaries

20   (2018, December 19): *"Over 85% of GCC listed companies have no female board member - study."* https://www.zawya.com/mena/en/markets/story/Over_85_of_GCC_listed_companies_have_no_female_board_member__study-ZAWYA20181219073818/

21   BBC News (2020, February 8): *"Women hold third of board roles at FTSE100 firms."* https://www.bbc.co.uk/news/business-51417469

22   The National (2016, March 8): *"Better, but room for improvement."* https://www.thenational.ae/uae/better-but-room-for-improvement-1.201936

23   Leone, M.J., Slezak, D.F., Golombek, D., Sigman, M. (2017). Time to Decide: Diurnal Variations on the Speed and Quality of Human Decisions. *Cognition*. doi: 10.1016/j.cognition.2016.10.007

24   www.oilandgasmiddleeast.com (2019, July 21): *"65% of UAE and Saudi Arabia's employees feel overworked: LinkedIn survey."* https://www.oilandgasmiddleeast.com/people/34598-65-of-uae-and-saudi-arabias-employees-feel-overworked-linkedin-survey

25   Siegel, D. (2011) *Mindsight: Transform Your Brain with the New Science of Kindness*. One World Publications.

26   Ipsos MORI & The Policy Institute, King's College, London (2019): *"Attitudes towards Mental Health in the United States and around the World."* https://www.kcl.ac.uk/news/four-in-five-say-mental-health-as-important-as-physical-but-just-one-in-five-think-nhs-treats-it-that-way

27   *"HR Careers Report 2019: Trends in titles, salaries and more."* https://library.namely.com/hr-careers-report-2019

28   Kahneman, D. (2013). *Thinking, Fast and Slow* (1st ed.). Farrar, Straus and Giroux.

29   Anthony Tomassini (2020, July 16): *"To make orchestras more diverse, end blind auditions."*
https://www.nytimes.com/2020/07/16/arts/music/blind-auditions-orchestras-race.html

and

Goldin, C., & Rouse, C. (2000). Orchestrating Impartiality: The Impact of "Blind" Auditions on Female Musicians. *The American Economic Review, 90*(4), 715-741.

30   Maureen Dowd (2018, September 8): *"Lady of the Rings: Jacinda Rules."*
https://www.nytimes.com/2018/09/08/opinion/sunday/jacinda-ardern-new-zealand-prime-minister.html

31   https://voxeu.org/article/women-leaders-are-better-fighting-pandemic 2020
https://voxeu.org/article/women-leaders-are-better-fighting-pandemic#.X0FTHv9BdSM.link

32   Collins, J. (2001). *Good to Great: Why Some Companies Make the Leap and Others Don't* (1st ed.). HarperBusiness EBook.

33   Wintrade Global Women Webinar Presenter, 9th July 2020. https://wintradeglobal.com/

34   Dweck, C. S. (2007). *Mindset: The New Psychology of Success* (Illustrated ed.). Ballantine Books.

35   Dubai School of Government Policy Brief: *Women's Leadership Development in the UAE* by Ghalia Gargani, May Al Dabbagh and Hannah Riley Bowles, (2012, December).

36   Ryan, R. M., & Deci, E. L. (2000). Self-determination theory and the facilitation of intrinsic motivation, social development, and well-being. *American Psychologist, 55*(1), 68–78. https://doi.org/10.1037/0003-066X.55.1.68

37   Sandberg, S. (2013). *Lean In: Women, Work, and the Will to Lead* (1st ed.). Knopf.

38   *Opening doors: gender equality and development in the Middle East and North Africa: Main report (English)*. MENA development report Washington, D.C.: World Bank Group (2013). http://documents.worldbank.org/curated/en/338381468279877854/Main-report

39   Assaad, Ragui A. and Hendy, Rana and Lassassi, Moundir and Yassin, Shaimaa (2018): *"Explaining the MENA Paradox: Rising Educational Attainment, Yet Stagnant Female Labor Force Participation."* IZA Discussion Paper No. 11385, Available at SSRN: https://ssrn.com/abstract=3153349

40   Schuller, T. (2017, March 12): *"Prisoners of the Paula Principle: why women work below their abilities."* https://www.theguardian.com/lifeandstyle/2017/mar/12/prisoners-of-the-paula-principle-women-work-below-abilities

41   www.arabianbusiness.com (2016, September 9): *Gulf SMEs led by women entrepreneurs worth $385bn* https://www.arabianbusiness.com/gulf-smes-led-by-women-entrepreneurs-worth-385bn-643830.html

42   United Nations Population Fund (UNFPA) (2017, May 10): *"New Survey shows violence against women widespread in Indonesia."* https://www.unfpa.org/news/new-survey-shows-violence-against-women-widespread-indonesia

43   Cialdini, R. B. (2006). *Influence: The Psychology of Persuasion, Revised Edition* (Revised ed.). HarperBusiness.

44   The Conversation (2020, July 7): *"Austerity in the Gulf states: why it's alarming for women's progress."* https://theconversation.com/austerity-in-the-gulf-states-why-its-alarming-for-womens-progress-142187

ABOUT THE AUTHOR

Annabel Harper MA is an Executive Leadership Coach and Facilitator, with a deep interest in the development of women in leadership in the Middle East. As part of her MA in Middle Eastern Studies at King's College, London, Annabel researched women's leadership in the United Arab Emirates. She holds an MA in Coaching & Mentoring Practice, a BSc (Soc Sci) Hons in Sociology and is a Fellow of the Royal Society of Arts.

Annabel has international experience in a variety of multi-cultural global organisations. Client sectors include FMCG, financial and professional services, pharma, broadcasting, government entities and business schools. As well as her coaching work, Annabel is a tutor on the Diploma in Coaching at the University of Cambridge Institute of Continuing Education. Previously, Annabel was a journalist at ITN, Channel 4 News and the BBC in the UK.

Annabel lives in Donegal, Ireland and Buckinghamshire, England with her husband and their two dogs.